ADOPTION
SEPARATION

Then and now

Evelyn Robinson

Clova Publications

ADOPTION SEPARATION

Published by

Clova Publications
PO Box 328
Christies Beach
South Australia 5165

www.clovapublications.com

© Evelyn Robinson, 2010

ISBN: 978-0-646-54874-6

By the same author:

Adoption and Loss – *The Hidden Grief*
ISBN: 78-0-646-43532-9

Adoption and Recovery – *Solving the mystery of reunion*
ISBN: 78-0-646-43370-7

Adoption Reunion – *Ecstasy or Agony?*
ISBN: 78-0-646-51697-4

Then and now

This book is dedicated to everyone, everywhere,

who has experienced adoption separation.

ADOPTION SEPARATION

CONTENTS

PART I: ***Adoption in the Twentieth Century***

Introduction
Australia
Canada
England
Ireland
New Zealand
Scotland
United States

PART II: ***Adoption in the Twenty-first Century***

Introduction
Picking up the pieces
Different approaches
In the country of daughters
The intercountry stolen generation
The Times They Are A-Changin'

ADOPTION SEPARATION

Adoption in the 20th century

ADOPTION SEPARATION

Then and now

Adoption separation, then

The first part of this book contains the narratives of parents who experienced adoption separation in the last century. They span a period of more than thirty years, from 1958 to 1989.

In the twentieth century, hundreds of thousands of children were adopted in the countries represented in this book, in circumstances very similar to the ones described here. It is difficult for members of the generations who did not live through this period to understand why so many adoptions occurred. I hope that reading the words of those who experienced adoption separation in the twentieth century will shed some light for them on the social environment of the era.

I have chosen not to try to explain the feelings expressed in this book, but to allow the stories to speak eloquently and powerfully for themselves. Readers who wish to gain a deeper understanding of the emotional issues around adoption separation and reunion could benefit from reading my other books.

Shame is a recurring theme in the narratives of those who have been separated from a family member by adoption. One definition of shame is: 'a painful feeling caused by an awareness of guilt'. The countries which are represented here have all been heavily influenced by the Judeo-Christian ethos, which traditionally attached shame and guilt to sexual relationships outside of marriage.

Pregnancy provided public evidence of the parents' sexual behaviour, which often exposed them to harsh judgment. This resulted in intense social pressure for adoptions to take place.

Shame can also be defined as: 'cause for regret'. Looking back, many now feel that it was a shame that so many adoptions occurred and many parents who have been separated from their children by adoption have expressed regret that they were unable to prevent the adoption from taking place.

I have been involved with post-adoption support services around the English-speaking world since 1986 and I have been struck over the years by the similarities in experiences in all of these countries. I decided that it would be useful to produce a book which would bring them together.

I sent requests for contributions to this book to friends, colleagues, acquaintances and to organisations. I requested that contributions be brief, in order to be able to include as many as possible. There is, of course, much more to all of these stories.

I know that it has been therapeutic for my contributors to have told their stories in their own words and that they feel that their experiences are validated by having them published. I am grateful for the enthusiasm, the courage and the generosity which they have brought to this project.

*This collection provides a vivid and moving picture of each parent's adoption experience and allows readers to understand exactly **how it happened**.*

Then and now

How it happened...

...in Australia

ADOPTION SEPARATION

Then and now

Alison's son was born in Australia in 1964

I was three weeks old when I was adopted from the Ballarat Children's Home and taken to live in Melbourne with my new parents and an older brother, who was also adopted. My new parents gave me every opportunity to experience life and the best of everything possible. I was told I was adopted from a very early age. However the reality of this information did not sink in until I was eleven years old.

I can remember being totally confused, angry and upset. There were so many questions and no answers. As I grew into my teenage years the need to know my 'real' mother became more and more intense. I realised that as far as my adoptive parents were concerned I was 'second best' – after all, if they had been able to have their own children, there would have been no interest in adopting any child.

Teenage years can be difficult, as we all try to search for our own identity. When you have been adopted, that identity is even harder to establish. Questions I asked myself were, 'Why was I given up?', 'What is my cultural background?', 'Who do I look like?' – the list goes on.

Just prior to turning sixteen, I wrote a promise to myself that I would find my 'real' mother by the time I was eighteen, or I would leave home. I hid this note behind a picture in my bedroom. Over the next few days I felt more and more guilty about being disloyal to my parents and went to retrieve the note, but, to my horror, the note had gone. This incident was never spoken of and I became increasingly nervous, believing I would be thrown out of home for showing my disloyalty; but this never happened.

ADOPTION SEPARATION

In 1964, when I was sixteen, I became pregnant. My parents shipped me off to Adelaide to a couple who took in unwed, pregnant girls to help with the domestic chores and look after their children. My boyfriend wasn't 'going to ruin his life' just because I was pregnant. As an adoptee, I was terrified of being abandoned and rejected and this experience confirmed my worst nightmares. I believed, as an adoptee, that I didn't deserve the best – if I had been good enough, I wouldn't have been given away. My parents blamed my birthmother for my sin – I came from 'bad blood'.

I spent the next six months feeling nothing. I was numb and in shock. I knew I couldn't keep my baby – that's not how things were done. It seemed completely normal to me to give my baby away – after all I had been given away too. During the pregnancy I received a 'phone call from a religious minister who asked if I would 'give' my child to a couple, parishioners of his church, who were past the age of being able to adopt through the normal channels, but were desperate for a child. He told me the woman had suffered more than ten miscarriages. I saw this as a way of payment for the free medical treatment and hospital costs provided by the Catholic community and agreed to 'donate' my child to this couple. From that time on, I felt like a surrogate mother. I was having a child for another couple. It never occurred to me that I could change my mind and certainly no one told me I could. At no time did I see a Social Worker, except to sign the adoption consent papers at the relevant Government office; nor was I advised of my rights. There was no responsible adult with me at the time of signing the adoption papers.

The birth of my baby was induced, due to the fact that my parents wanted me home for Christmas, so that my absence didn't have to be explained. I was completely naïve regarding the birth procedure but, as it turned out, it didn't matter, as I was drugged from beginning to end. The only thing I knew was that I had given birth to a boy and that he was healthy.

Then and now

I never saw him and I never asked to see him. I didn't believe I deserved to ask any questions. I spent the next seven days alone in a hospital room, not having any visitors and visited rarely by the nurses.

I returned home to Melbourne and life went on. I started working and married the father of my child, because I didn't think anyone else would want me. We went on to have two daughters, but the marriage failed and my ex-husband fought for custody of the girls. Again, I simply gave them away, because that's what you do. They were eight and eleven years old at the time. I didn't even cry when they left, much to the shock of my friends, who expected me to be distraught, but I had done it before and knew how to cope, by simply becoming numb and blocking out any emotions.

The need to find my birth family was still great and when the *Victorian Adoption Act (1984)* became legislation, I joined the queue of thousands wanting their records. I waited four years for my number to come up. When I am asked what is the best day in my life, my immediate reply is, "The day I received my birth records." I was euphoric. I don't think I stopped smiling for days. What blew me away was the fact that I had been given a name. I hadn't named my son. No one told me I could. It took me a week to trace my natural family, but I was devastated when I discovered that my birthmother had passed away in 1974 – the year of my youngest daughter's birth.

But then the sorrow turned to joy, as I discovered I had two sisters, one older and one younger and they wanted to meet me. This relationship is still continuing. I am a full member of the family, attend Christmases, birthdays, weddings, anniversaries and, sadly, funerals. Although we are separated by distance, we talk on the 'phone constantly. My older sister said, "My only regret is that we missed out on knowing you for forty years."

In the same year that I reunited with my birth family, my adoptive brother passed away from bone cancer. I then felt the need to find my son. I wanted to give him the chance to meet his birthmother while I was still alive, to let him know the circumstances of his adoption and to find out if he was well and happy.

I applied for the birth records from the South Australian Government Department but chose not to begin searching at that time. I was too busy trying to assimilate my new family into my life and grieving for the loss of my brother. It wasn't until 1996, after the death of my adoptive father at the age of ninety-two, that I began the search. As luck would have it, my son is a computer freak and so it only took a quick search on Google to find him. I wrote an outreach letter to him and had a positive reply back within two days. I arranged to fly to Adelaide for the weekend to meet him for the first time. I was absolutely terrified at the prospect of having to explain to him why I had given him away. At our first meeting he reached out to me to give me a hug – I couldn't respond and so I inadvertently pushed him away. We spent the weekend together, but the strain this put on both of us was huge and it was a relief for us both to say goodbye at the airport.

On arriving back in Melbourne, I couldn't stop crying. I cried for five days. All that grief that I had never allowed myself to feel came out and I didn't have the strength to stop it. I eventually sought help and spent the next two years having intensive counselling. I was diagnosed with post traumatic stress disorder. My son and I corresponded by e-mail but after a few months I realised that he didn't want to keep up contact. He told me that he had agreed to meet with me purely to satisfy his curiosity and having done that, he wanted nothing more from me. He was not angry, understood my lack of choice at the time and had never felt 'different' because he was adopted. He had a happy childhood and had no regrets, but even knowing all this, I still felt rejected. However, I accepted his decision and let him know that, if he changed his mind, I would welcome him.

Thirteen years passed and then, one day, while I was on a Mediterranean cruise, my daughter received a message on Facebook from my son's wife. She thought he was now ready for a relationship. Needless to say, I was extremely wary, as I knew I couldn't go through the heartbreak again. To cut a long story short, my son and I are now slowly building trust between one another. He and his family live in Arizona, USA and so distance prevents us from personal contact, but I am hopeful that he and his family will return to Australia one day. I have a beautiful granddaughter whom I have yet to meet, but I'm patient – I can wait.

Reunion with my son put the smile back on my dial and I now feel content. All the loose family ends have been tied together and while we all have our own lives and are separated by distance, we are connected for life. It's been a long, hard road with many lessons to be learned along the way, but the end result has led to feelings of inner peace – feelings I treasure and will hold on to for as long as possible.

~~~

Hannah's son was born in Australia in 1964

Having spent a small fortune on psychotherapy fees, not to mention the time, effort and emotional energy I expended over a six year period, I finally discovered that harbouring secrets can cause greater damage than the actual 'crime' that's been committed. The amount of energy it takes to repress the truth to conceal the real level of grief that lies within, ultimately takes its toll.

Part of the psychotherapy journey involved stripping away the layers of protection that had accumulated over the years, so that some sense of normality could be projected to the outside world. Without those protective layers, it was impossible to face the daily grind of life. However, now that those layers of protective covering have been torn away, it has exposed another 'me' that I have to face and let others know about, or at least those that matter.

I learned to face the undeniable truth that by the time I was eighteen years old, the damage to my psyche had been firmly established, whereby I felt entirely worthless, with no self-esteem and lacking any confidence. I have come to understand and accept that my ageing parents did the best they could with the resources they had, but, unfortunately, their parenting skills were sadly lacking and, consequently, I literally fell into the arms of the first man who came along who showed me some sign of affection and much to my dismay found myself pregnant.

At the time, I was working in my mother's factory without receiving any wages, one of the many ventures she embarked on over the years and I had no money to deal with an unplanned pregnancy. I slipped into a state of denial hoping that 'things would eventually right themselves'. Unfortunately, they didn't.

After thirteen weeks I finally made an appointment to see a doctor who confirmed my worst fears. I was too scared to procure a back-yard abortion because of newspaper stories that I'd read that often detailed the gruesome consequences, but I didn't have the money to approach the few doctors who performed the procedure, albeit illegally. In any event, the doctor told me it was too late, as it was in those days, being 1964.

The father of my child had found someone else by this time and I was left penniless and pregnant, living in a dysfunctional family environment.

A friend of my child's father, M, took pity on me and offered to take me to Sydney for the remainder of my pregnancy, agreeing that adoption was the best option for everyone concerned.

I kept hoping that some miracle would happen and I would be able to keep my baby, but no such miracle took place.

Except for the midwives, who were mostly kind to me, if not somewhat distant, I laboured on my own for twenty-seven hours and at the moment of birth, the midwife held a pillow in front of my face, so that I wouldn't see the baby I had carried for nine months.

Although this action was punitive, I also knew in my heart that, if I ever laid eyes on my baby, I would never be able to go through with the adoption.

After the birth, I was transferred to the post-natal ward, where I stayed for a day or so, among five other young mothers whose babies were brought out from the nursery every few hours to be fed. All I could do was turn my head away, so that I wouldn't see these young married women, feeding and cradling their babies.

I was then transferred to an Annex that belonged to the Crown Street Women's Hospital, where I recall the Social Worker visiting me three days after the birth. She stood at my bedside until I signed the Consent Form for Adoption. I applied for my medical records from the Crown Street Women's Hospital years later and discovered that I was given large doses of drugs the night before and the morning of signing the consent form for adoption. Also the legislation required a five day interval between the time of birth and obtaining consent. However, my signature was obtained on the third day.

Despite my desperation in wanting to keep my baby, I knew that I couldn't bring this child back into my mother's dysfunctional home to experience the same irrational and damaging behaviour I had known all my life. Unfortunately, my sisters' circumstances weren't that much better, despite their offers of assistance and M had made it perfectly clear that he would also disappear, unless I came home alone. I was told many years later that there was a Commonwealth Benefit available that I was eligible to apply for, but I was not told about it by the Social Worker who was involved in the adoption process.

They say 'life's full of choices', but there was really only one choice for me and that was to sign the consent form to allow an adoption to proceed. I recall the social worker telling me to 'forget all about it' and work to make a new life for myself 'as if it never happened.' That was the extent of my 'grief counselling', not only for me, but also for tens of thousands of other young women who were shameless and disgraceful enough to become pregnant out of wedlock. I think I have some inkling of what the term 'stolen generation' means.

I did as I was told and what I thought was expected of me and tried to 'forget all about it'. When M proposed, I agreed to marry him, because I believed that no self-respecting man would look at me once he knew of 'my past'.

The layers of protection had begun to be laid, the lies, the denial, the suppression of grief for the loss of this child, all became part of 'forgetting all about it...as if it never happened'.

Within a short period of time the social landscape changed immeasurably and young women were not only having babies out of wedlock, but also received financial assistance to help them provide for their offspring. The legislation also changed enabling reunions to take place and so in 1982 when my 'baby' turned eighteen, I registered with Adoption Triangle in case he ever wanted to search for his birthmother.

Life goes on and despite the arrival of three other children, a divorce from M and a re-marriage 'the secret' remained buried.

I heard nothing until 1986, when my husband and I returned from an overseas trip. A letter was waiting from Adoption Triangle. I was thrown into an absolute spin, because I had done such a magnificent job keeping this part of my life so secret, that even my husband and other children didn't know of my first child's existence.

After I broke the news to my husband, he offered to make the initial contact as an intermediary and arranged to meet with my son who had been named Peter by his adoptive parents. His then fiancée was also present. Peter was twenty-two years old. My husband reported that all Peter wanted was some information about his medical history and to exchange photos. My husband brought back a photo of my 'baby' who had matured into a young adult. After that meeting I wrote Peter a long letter explaining the circumstances that led to his birth and subsequent adoption and told him of my profound sorrow at having to relinquish him. I received no reply.

Then in 1989 when my 'eldest' son Anthony was diagnosed with a particularly virulent form of bone cancer, 'my past' really came back to haunt me. I can still recall the moment when I heard the word 'malignancy' mentioned, that my immediate reaction was *this is my punishment for giving away my first born son* and in that same split second I knew that I was also destined to lose Anthony.

Within two years Anthony had succumbed to the ravages of his disease and I was overcome with grief at his loss.

In 1996, some five years after his death, I still found myself shedding buckets of tears. The very mention of his name opened up the tear ducts, as if there was no tomorrow and I found myself weeping, yet again.

I was finally persuaded to have some grief counselling. I tentatively took myself off to see a psychotherapist, terrified out of my wits that I would let my defences down and was unable to cope with the thought of revealing 'the secret'.

After a couple of sessions talking about Anthony's illness, the therapist asked me to record my dreams. I attended my third session, carrying pages full of the previous week's dreams, one of which had the Federal Police standing at my front door, asking if I knew the identity of a man whose body had been discovered in a nearby river. I told them I didn't know who he was. The therapist asked if I knew anyone whose initials were FP or PF (Federal Police). However, no-one came to mind at the time.

He asked me to keep the letters in mind, as the name may come to me later.

The following weekend I was reading the Sunday paper in which there was an article about all the children left abandoned in Romanian orphanages. Then, like a bolt of lightening, I suddenly realised the meaning of my dream.

Through my work, I was aware of an experienced paediatric nurse whose initials were PF, who had left her job in Melbourne and travelled to Romania to work in one of those orphanages, looking after abandoned children – just like the child I had abandoned all those years ago.

What's that other saying? 'You can run but you can't hide.' I could no longer run from 'the secret', because, if I was going to grieve properly over my loss of Anthony, I had to first learn how to grieve over my loss of Peter – something I had never been allowed to do by others or myself.

At the therapist's suggestion I wrote to Peter again at the end of 1996 and met him for the first time in early 1997. Despite having been given all the trappings in life, I found him to be 'troubled', although a great actor, trying to pretend that everything was just fine – a familiar trait! We met again a few times after that, including one occasion when he met his half-sister and brother. However, he has been reluctant to keep in contact with us and in the meantime has married and become the father of two children.

After much soul-searching, I think I've come to accept that I may never again see the son I lost to adoption or his family, because, although he can intellectualise the reasons behind his adoption, it doesn't alter the fact that 'I gave him away' and though he may never want to acknowledge me as his birthmother, he will always be my son, no matter how much he may want to deny it.

As a 'relinquishing' mother I continue to grapple with the lasting effects of that event that took place almost forty-six years ago and, as time passes, the grief and pain inflicted by that *primal wound* have not diminished. In fact, these feelings have worsened with the passage of time, like any other incident of post-traumatic stress.

I have found that it is ultimately easier to come to terms with losing a child to cancer than losing a child to adoption. When a child dies, society joins with you to mourn your loss. There are rituals that allow you to grieve publicly, such as a funeral service and a grave to visit, where it's possible to retain some physical and spiritual connection. With time, it's possible to achieve a sense of peace and acceptance.

Despite the oft-repeated words of the social worker to 'forget all about it … as if it never happened', it's a fallacy to think that anyone can simply walk away without recognising and acknowledging the life-long impact of adoption.

There does come a time when we do have to move on, but, equally we need to be able to do so honestly and openly, so there is no longer a need to hide behind a veil of secrecy.

~~~~

Roslyne's son was born in Australia in 1964

In 1963, at the age of seventeen and a half, I became pregnant.

I refused to marry the father and so my parents, with the encouragement of the local GP, arranged for me to enter Kate Cocks Home for Unmarried Mothers in Brighton, South Australia. I would live there until the baby was born, leave the baby there and then arrive home as if I was returning from working in the country. Because of my great shame and fear of being 'found out', I went along with all these lies.

The lies continued when I resigned from work and told my colleagues that I was going to the country for work. This is also the story my parents told to family, friends and neighbours, before I entered the Home. I lived in fear of someone coming to the house and seeing me before I had time to hide somewhere. It was obviously a very stressful time for both my baby and me.

I entered the Home two months before my son was born. Before I entered the Home, I had to have a chest x-ray, in case I had tuberculosis. I also had to give a faecal sample, to ensure that I didn't have a sexually transmitted disease. All of this ensured that I felt like a very bad girl when I finally did arrive at the Home.

My first duty was to visit the matron in charge of the Home. She informed me that, to protect my anonymity, I could not use my given name, but would have to choose another. This didn't seem unusual to me at that time, as there had been so many preceding lies up until then, that it just seemed normal. I chose the name 'Lyn' and I became another person. I think this may have been what helped get me through that time I spent in the Home.

After this meeting, I was shown to my room in the dormitory and then sent to assist the nurses in the children's Home. From then on, I worked, unpaid, six days a week in the kitchen, laundry, childcare centre, garden and nurses' home and, if we'd had any training as a nurse, we even worked in the hospital where our babies were born.

When we were rostered in the kitchen, we prepared meals for the nursing staff, who made it pretty clear what they thought of us. I can remember there was an elderly lady living in the dormitory with us who, I think now, may have been a social worker. She used to call us into her room occasionally to sign forms. I presume it was to obtain our unemployment benefits from the government, which went towards the fees we had to pay each week to the Home. We were never given any help or advice from her, though, on how to keep our babies. We were so conditioned to the fact that we were going to leave without our babies that we never even asked about alternatives to adoption for our children. We just presumed there weren't any. It was made perfectly clear to us from the beginning, that there would not be any support from our families or the government if we kept our babies.

So here we were – a bunch of society outcasts, brainwashed into submission and suffering feelings of such low esteem and low self worth, that I can say it has had an impact on every decision I have made in life since.

In January, 1964, after a long and difficult birth, my son was born. The week prior to his birth, I was told by the nursing sister that my blood pressure was very high, but, because most of us had little or no knowledge about pregnancy and its inherent dangers, I didn't worry about it. The nursing sister didn't suggest bed rest or taking it easy and so I carried on working as normal, until the day I went into labour.

We were always worried that we would have difficult births, that required us to be rushed, haemorrhaging, to the Queen Victoria Hospital in Adelaide. It happened occasionally and we'd heard horror stories from those girls who worked in the hospital that the general mode of transport in this instance was in the back of the Home's station wagon.

We were warned that we would not see our baby after it was born, but the matron who assisted at the delivery was worried about me and let me nurse my son. I did develop toxaemia and so was sedated and confined to bed for about five days afterwards. All I can remember of that time was the matron waking me up through the night to take my blood pressure and administer more sedation, whilst the mothers and a nursing sister attended to me during the day.

On the seventh day, I was able to get up and move around. The Deaconess called me into the waiting room. She said, "I have a form for you to sign." She then asked me if there was any request I had of the adopting parents. All I could think to say was, "Don't make him learn the piano if he doesn't want to." She then asked me if I wanted to name the baby. I said I didn't want to remember a name, thinking it would somehow be easier if she named him instead. She said she would name him after her own husband and wrote down his name. She then handed the form to me to sign, without covering up the names she had just given my baby, 'Brenton Ronald' – and that was it.

I was never informed of any of my rights. I know now that if I had changed my mind within thirty days, I could have kept my baby. I don't know if my parents were even aware of this at the time. The Methodist Church who ran this home was running an efficient adoption agency for their parishioners. The family who adopted my baby eventually adopted three children through Kate Cocks Home.

I stayed in the hospital for two weeks and, during that time, could hear babies crying, but was told that I was not allowed to go anywhere near the nursery. I, of course, obeyed the rules, even though I knew when one of the babies crying was mine. The young mothercraft nurse who looked after our babies felt really bad about how we were treated, but obviously felt powerless to disobey the rules. I made contact with her after I reunited with my son and discovered that she has suffered dreadful guilt feelings since.

I feel really angry now when I realise that I could have gone down to the nursery, picked my baby up and walked out. My mother was allowed to go and see him. She said to me, "Don't make me do that again or we won't be able to leave him here." How stupid of me. Obviously, she was weakening, but I wasn't aware that I had any rights to my own baby.

After two weeks, I was able to go home. I was given tablets to dry up my milk and told to go home, 'forget about it' and get on with my life. I followed these instructions and I now believe it would have destroyed me if I hadn't. The family never mentioned 'it' and I went along with this silence for many years.

It was only when I had my daughter and son later on, that I understood what had been stolen from me, but to survive mentally, I had to put it to the back of my mind.

Due to the laws of our land, I couldn't search for my son until he turned eighteen and so I just had to grieve in private. Even my husband didn't seem to have any understanding of what I was going through.

I attempted to search for my son when he turned eighteen, but, because there weren't any support groups to assist me, I didn't really know what to do. So, once again, it was put to the back of my mind and I continued to 'get on with my life'. One of the places I contacted was the Methodist Mission who owned Kate Cocks Home. I received a hostile reception there; I was told to stop searching and that a fire had destroyed all the records anyway. I had hoped to follow up my medical history, but that put an end to that pursuit. A social worker from the Department of Community Welfare also contacted me and told me to stop looking for my son and not to contact the Mission again.

In 1985, when my son was twenty-two, I started searching again. This time, due to suggestions from another mother, I searched the electoral rolls and birth notices from the year he was born and believed I had found my son. I contacted the Department of Family and Community Services and told them I had found my son and requested their help in reuniting with him. This did cause a slight problem, because I had actually found an adopted boy who had been born on the same day as my own son.

Because of this, my case worker decided to tell me that they had had contact over the years with my son's adoptive mother, who wanted my son to be reunited with me. Because my son hadn't requested contact himself, they could only write to him on my behalf and ask him if he would like to meet me. I was told that he didn't reply to the letter and so the social worker handling his file at the time decided not to·bother any more and filed it away at the bottom of the pile.

Fortunately, as a result of my locating the wrong child, they decided that I should have contact with my son, before I caused any more trouble for them. This is where my search ended. I was finally given my son's address, so that I could write to him myself. After receiving a letter back from him, the Department decided that we could reunite with each other.

We were reunited in March, 1986. It was twenty-three years after my son's birth. The reunion was not what I had hoped it would be. My son lives in a country town in South Australia and was very laid back about his adoption. He was not too bothered about meeting me and had stipulated that if we met, then I'd have to travel to him. Generally the reunions were on neutral ground, but this one was in his house, with his adoptive family present. His adoptive father was cold towards me and clearly disapproved of our reunion. However his adoptive mother was lovely, because the reunion was what she had hoped for.

My son is now forty-six and married with two beautiful children. It has only been in the last few years that I have finally begun to 'be myself' with him. He understands why we were separated by adoption and holds no animosity towards me. Since our reunion, I have attended various counselling sessions but find it is easier just to try to accept it.

It is now very clear to me that, after my son's birth, I was denied the opportunity to express the normal feelings of anger, hurt and emotional pain and it has left me with an aching void which will never be filled again.

~~~~

Glennys's daughter was born in Australia in 1966

In 1966, in Perth, Western Australia, I gave birth to a baby girl. I could not keep her and had to relinquish her to adoption.

Then and now

I remember buying a fake wedding ring, so that people wouldn't stare at me when I went on the bus to the hospital for a check up.

My mother couldn't help me, as she was a widow since I was eight and so I had to get a job being a home help for a rich woman, who only allowed me to eat what she said I could. I felt a burden to everyone and so when my sister took me in for the last few weeks, I tried to do everything I could to pay for my board by doing all her housework and cooking. In those days, we received no help from the government and I didn't want to end up in a home for unmarried mothers.

I hid away as much as possible and so didn't go to visit my mother; if the neighbours had seen me it would have embarrassed her. When I gave birth, I was dropped at the hospital, as my sister had to work. I spent the thirty hours' labour mostly by myself, except the last few with a trainee doctor, who had to go for help when it became obvious that I wasn't going to give birth without help.

I didn't see my baby and neither did my mother, who wanted to, but the social worker wasn't there to give permission. I was in a ward with other women who had their babies, until they moved me to a room in a small house owned by the hospital. No one ever spoke about it. My brother-in-law wouldn't let me talk about it and told me to forget it and get on with my life.

The thing that hurts the most is that I have just found out that there was support for us to keep our babies in 1966, but no one advised us of its availability.

To think I have been through years of not knowing and now not being able to have contact, which could have been avoided, devastates me. Thankfully I have a wonderful husband and two children to make up in a small way for what I have lost.

ADOPTION SEPARATION

Pamela's son was born in Australia in 1967

This is the story of my three mothers and of the impact of the adoption process on our lives. You can draw your own conclusions as to what their stories reveal and what we need to be aware of.

My first mother, whom I'll call Lily, thought that she would be married to my father and therefore keep the child she was pregnant with. This was not to be. The marriage did not take place and she was unable to keep me. When I was six days old, she had to hand me over to my adoptive parents. It was her twenty-first birthday. She was utterly devastated.

I have only a faint memory of my second mother, Nell. I never truly bonded with her. Nell was quite simply the wrong mother; she wasn't a bad mother – just the wrong one, although I obviously couldn't articulate this at the time. She didn't smell right, her voice was the wrong voice, her rhythms were the wrong rhythms, her interests, talents and tendencies were very different from mine and the attunement which most mothers feel was simply not there. My recollections of Nell are hazy at best. The few photos I have are no help: it's as if I'm looking at a stranger.

I have absolutely no experience of warm, embracing, truly connected motherly love. I just don't know what that feels like. I'm ashamed to say that I feel envious of people who do know.

Although I always felt closer to my Dad, I was like an alien in my adoptive family. My Dad, in fact, used to say that I was 'different' – what a loaded word and how true that was! I was a passionate child with an obvious talent for music, dancing and art, with an 'artistic temperament' – totally foreign to everyone in my extended adoptive family. My Dad used to say that I felt things 'too deeply'. Nevertheless I know that he loved me dearly, even though I was a mystery to him.

Nell was hospitalised when I was eleven and died when I was thirteen – not exactly the best time to lose your mother –

whether first, second or third! Again, this is something that's never mentioned when talking about adoption. Nobody ever says that the family might break up, one of the parents might die, or leave or divorce – which for the child can feel like yet another abandonment.

So to mother number three, whom I'll call Margot. She was the best of a series of comical housekeepers we had after the death of mother number two. There was quite a rapid turnover – I think about six in eighteen months. Finally, along came Margot: dark-eyed, energetic, smart, an ex-nurse, good cook and organiser.

She was an excellent housekeeper, but she was emotionally fragile. She could be really kind and sweet, but was also highly unpredictable. You never knew how she would respond to anything. She could be violent and angry, especially after drinking alcohol. There was something about her that disturbed me; we never really got on. Although my Dad married her, I sensed that she was jealous of his love for me. It was Margot who told me, in a fit of anger one day when my Dad was out of the house, that I was adopted. I was seventeen years old at the time.

Some twelve years after they married, I became pregnant and was determined to keep my baby son – my first and only blood relative. I tried valiantly for some thirteen months, (including breast-feeding him for five months while working in the theatre). Towards the end of that time, I lived in a house with four gay men, who were absolutely wonderful in helping me care for him. Because of the nature of my work as an actress, there were lots of complicated arrangements involved. Eventually the stress of working in two plays (day and night) became too much. My Dad came to visit, saw my predicament and suggested that I come home to live.

It was a total disaster. Margot was worse than ever: dangerous and scary. I was absolutely desperate and the huge strain of living in a house with a baby and an unpredictable and sometimes violent woman began seriously to affect both my mental health and my baby. I sought help from two people I respected very much. Both told me that in the best interests of my son, I should give him up to a couple who could give him what I could not: a secure home and a father. 'Every boy needs a father!', apparently.

By this stage, my sense of self worth was at rock bottom: I had no money and no work (there was no government payment for single parents at this time) and I was living in a dangerous environment. I agonised for weeks, but all the time this situation was affecting my child. The last straw was seeing a very dear nun at my old school, who, of course, said the same as all the others. My stepmother was becoming more unpredictable and crazy. I had come to the end of the road and so I did the unthinkable.

My Dad came with me and afterwards I went away by myself and grieved and sobbed and cried for ten days, against all advice, I must say. I believe that doing that saved my sanity. Most mothers were not permitted to grieve; they were told...'forget about it, put it behind you and get on with your life'. As if we could!

I was in contact with the social worker who had arranged the adoption and who knew the family. The father apparently was very understanding; he was a practising psychiatrist and I was told that he was very fond of my little boy, who had taken to him as well. I subsequently found out that this father died when my son was four years old and so not only did he experience yet another abandonment, but the one chance he had to form an attachment to a father figure was lost to him.

He ended up being raised by a single mother anyway and one who understood him far less than I would have done. The fact that I was not told still makes my blood boil.

Many years later, I met my first mother, Lily, again, after an initial reluctance on her part. I then met my half brother and sister and other family members. Everything was wonderful –

until I wanted to know my father's name. Lily was not happy: she didn't want to tell me, but eventually she wrote the name on a piece of paper and said that she didn't want to hear any more about it.

A few years later when I was being interviewed for an article in a popular magazine, the journalist – a well known and highly respected member of her profession – asked me if I had met my father. I told her that under no circumstances was she to print that I had; this was strictly off the record, as my mother would be most upset. That journalist – in a gross breach of journalistic ethics – printed what I had said. A family member who had disapproved of my 'turning up' told my mother about the article and from that day onwards Lily never spoke to me again. That was over twenty years ago. She died last year, still refusing to speak to me.

I firmly believe that this was the result of the pain of having to give me up. I am forever associated with that pain – I'm my father's daughter and Lily could never forgive me for wanting to find that part of my heritage.

I've since found out that she was a very determined woman, but, according to an older sister, it was the impact of having to give me up which had resulted in a marked change in her personality. From then on she had to be in total control of everything in her life, even if it damaged her relationships with other people. I find I still grieve for our lost time and for the fact that she could not find it in her heart to reconnect with me.

I finally made my peace with her and attended her memorial service when she died.

My dear brother had included me in the eulogy; an act of generosity and acceptance which still takes my breath away. At the end of the service, my beautiful son was one of the casket bearers. We then all mingled at a nearby café where, once again, I found myself looking for – and finding – those family resemblances that are so very precious to all adopted people.

ADOPTION SEPARATION

My father's story was very different from the one Lily had told me, but just as devastating. I don't know what the truth is and never will. His response to me was very different: 'How is Lily? Is she happy? Does she have a good life?' When I met his daughter, my sister, she said that he was the most wonderful, loving, kind father one could wish for, who adored his children and always had time for them. Was this, I wonder, his response to what had happened? He had fathered a child and then, apparently, abandoned the mother. Was he trying to make up for this in some way?

Some time after mother number three, stepmother Margot, died, I discovered something that I believe explained her bizarre and sometimes frightening behaviour. Had we known at the time, perhaps things could have been different. She too had been forced to give up her daughter for adoption. This explained her peculiar and alarming ways. She was literally mad with unexpressed grief and rage, I think and when she was confronted with me doing what she had been prevented from doing ie raising my son as a single mother, she could not tolerate it.

Also, she was living in a house containing an adopted daughter – a reminder every day of what had happened to her own child. The daughter she lost to adoption had, sadly, died before they could meet, but Margot had been in contact with her granddaughter. Yet another example of the on-going negative and devastating effects of the adoption process. It truly seems to be never-ending.

Our stories must be told, so that people fully understand the on-going implications of the adoption process.

The process of adoption is damaging in and of itself and the task of the adopted person is to understand and hopefully reverse the psychic harm we have suffered and to become the authentic selves we have lost. Thankfully, while this is a long and difficult process, it is not impossible – with the help of those who are willing and, most importantly, able to help us along the way.

Then and now

Emma's son was born in Australia in 1968

The general public have no idea of the pain so many of us have endured. How do you tell people of your pain and suffering? Betrayal is what I have felt over the years. I could not even begin to tell people my story; it is too long.

So many of our children who have been adopted say, "Yes, we understand it was different back then." However, it is difficult for them really to understand our loss and many still harbour feelings of abandonment.

During my pregnancy, I was living with different people, who did not care about me and only wanted my money. I had to look after their children and had only a camper bed to sleep on. That and much more was my lot. Doctors spoke down to me, never comforting me. Years later I discovered that the very doctor who was looking after me actually had a sister, whom he had helped to adopt two children.

I find it hard to understand how so many parents pressured their children to give up their babies for adoption and then failed to recognise the heartache of losing a child. In my case, my mother was raised in a home and had a terrible upbringing. She was separated from both of her children, because they were taken into care. Mum died in 1992 and I have very little knowledge of her life. When my son was born, Mum was never given the opportunity to see her grandchild, although she knew that she was a grandmother. She was brought to the hospital, only to be told that she had no rights again. My mother was dismissed as both a mother to myself and a grandmother to my son.

After the birth of my son, when I left the hospital, I discovered that my mother herself was in hospital, having suffered a nervous breakdown. I visited her regularly and for the first month she did not recognise me, due to sedation. At the time, I felt that I could not grieve the loss of my child, because I had to be strong for her, but I was angry with the treatment of my mother and now feel very sad for her. After three months, my mother began to come to terms with the loss of her grandchild. However, I feel that she carried that loss with her for the rest of her life.

My own blessing was when my mother was close to passing away. I had found my son, but he had not yet met my mother. She asked me if she could go. I was unable to answer her, but she knew that I was not ready for her to die and, two weeks later, my son came to visit his adoptive mother and visited me also. I asked that he visit my mother, which he agreed to do. Whilst Mum was apprehensive, she rose from her bed, let go of my hand, smiled at John and asked if he would come to see her again. I have only one photograph of my mother, myself and her grandson together and I treasure it.

I visited Mum again just after she had met my son and she again told me that she was tired and I knew what she meant. With tears in my eyes and heart, I said, "Yes, Mum, you can go now." Two weeks later Mum died, but at least I had some peace, knowing that she had finally been able to meet her grandson, after being denied the opportunity when he was born.

When children are lost to adoption, the whole family experiences that loss.

~~~~

Carmel's son was born in Australia in 1970

[This statement was made by MP Michelle Roberts, Member for Midland, in the Western Australian Parliament, for the Adoption Apology debate, 19th. October, 2010. It was kindly provided by Carmel.]

Over past years, in less enlightened times, tens of thousands of women have lost their children to adoption. If the truth were to be fully acknowledged, it wouldn't take much scratching of the social fabric to find adoption experiences in many families.

Carmel is present here today. Her only child was born in September, 1970.

Due to the prejudice of the time, he was registered as an 'unnamed' child on his original birth certificate. This was contrary to Carmel's wish, but she was dissuaded from naming him. She was told, "It doesn't matter; the adoptive parents will give him a new name anyway." Documents released from his file many years after his birth are titled: "Notification of Illegitimate Child" and stamped in bold letters denoting him as being "ILLEGITIMATE". His father was listed on the original birth certificate as 'not stated'.

Carmel sees this now as an administrative convenience by those facilitating the relinquishment process. The father was denied the opportunity to acknowledge paternity of the child, thereby excluding him and simplifying the relinquishment process. Carmel was able to have her son's original birth certificate corrected in 2000 to show his name as "Charles Edward Peter". He has declined contact with Carmel.

Pregnant, unmarried women were scorned; their children were referred to as bastards and branded as 'illegitimate'. The relinquishment formalities were generally conducted with the mother under considerable duress, within a relatively short time after the birth, with limited options for the mothers and the high probability of rejection by her family if she chose to keep the child. Generally no efforts were made to allow women to bond with their baby. Some, like Carmel, were given the limited opportunity to hold their baby at the time of the birth. Many did not see their babies. The adoption process, either by misguided altruism or blatant conspiracy, made these so-called 'unwanted' and 'unnamed' babies into a desirable commodity.

The supply of children was used by the 'adoption system' principally to satisfy the demand for babies for infertile couples. Not all babies were adopted and not all went to childless couples.

Some went to families as a replacement child for a still-born baby, or where a baby had died shortly after birth.

The adoption process severed the legal rights of the mothers and the children were given new identities. Some were not told about being adopted and many were actively discouraged from searching for their family of origin. These women were, by and large, deemed not accepted or worthy of the title of 'Mother'.

This has caused a deep pain and sadness for them. Mother's Day is hardly a cause for them to celebrate. There are diverse views about the term to be used to describe the women who lost children to adoption: relinquishing mother, natural mother, first mother, birth mother, original mother. These women gave their child the greatest gift; the gift of life. The mothers who lost their children to adoption were told to forget about the baby and get on with their lives, ie NOT to be a mother. The event was not to be mentioned again by the mother, the family, friends and certainly not mentioned in polite society.

These women suffered disenfranchised grief; their loss was not acknowledged, their grief was unspoken and the mothers were unsupported. Counselling and emotional support were generally not available and their loss was definitely not understood. These mothers remember the birthdays of their lost children, often observing other people's children for the milestones of growth and development – always with the sense of renewed loss and grief. Having other children didn't diminish the loss or replace the child. Many women have suffered deep depression throughout their lives, their sense of loss and grief increasing with time.

The irony is that some suffered further; they were not able to have other children for a wide range of reasons. Again, this has added to their sense of loss.

The circumstances of the women who lost children to adoption differ widely, but the loss suffered by them is immeasurable.

Then and now

Loz's son was born in Australia in 1970

At the age of thirteen, I was molested by my uncle, a trusted relative, who gave me my first orgasm. I was shocked and didn't know what had happened. He threatened me and told me not to tell anyone. I later found out that he had also molested my younger sister.

At the age of fifteen, I was caught out doing a bit of heavy petting in the back yard by my Dad. Not long after that, I was simply dropped off at the St Kilda police station and taken to the Good Shepherd Convent for a couple of years, because I was 'uncontrollable'. Meanwhile my two brothers and one sister were locked up from society in institutions. This has ruined all of our lives.

Not long after I was released from the convent, I was raped by two Italian boys in a car, then thrown out near my home. I met these guys through a girlfriend and we went visiting a few friends. When it was time to go, my girlfriend and I got into the car to go home. She was dropped off and all I can remember is fighting them off.

I had my arm through the steering wheel and I told them I had a venereal disease (although I didn't) and they still proceeded. I had to give in or else I would have been seriously injured. I didn't tell anyone except my brother and, a week after the incident, I went to the police. I was the criminal, because they didn't believe me.

I went a bit wild after that and hitchhiked up North with two girlfriends, as far away as possible from home. I was still naïve and not using any contraception. After several months, I found out that I was pregnant. When I was five months' pregnant, I came home to face the music. I was once again locked away from society, living with a doctor's family in Brighton.

I hated living there and finally I rang up the convent. The convent accepted me back and I was locked away from everyone;

no contact was to be made with any of the other girls in the convent.

Soon after that, I went and stayed with a family at Beaumaris, until I gave birth to my son, Peter. He was born at the Royal Women's Hospital and there were student doctors and nurses everywhere, as if I was an experiment. It was a forceps delivery and very painful and I had lots of stitches. They took Peter away and I saw him once only after that, in his crib. I don't remember if I got to hold him. They put me in a horrible ward, which was like a lean-to, right on the main road. All I can remember is a lot of pain and only one visitor. I think I was put as far away from the maternity ward as possible.

I never really drank much until after Peter's birth. I went home and it was business as usual. I got a job, as if nothing had happened. Then I went to work in the snowfields, still without any support or knowledge and got pregnant again.

This time I left there when I was about three months' pregnant. I couldn't face my parents and went straight to Adelaide to catch up with the father again. He didn't really believe it was his, but he helped me out a little bit financially, until I got a job as a waitress in a strip club in Hindley Street.

I worked right up until the day Iann was born and had a couple of weeks off to rest, then back to work as a waitress again. I was severely depressed, but didn't know it, prior to Iann being born. I had a lot of pressure from one of the prostitutes that worked in the club to give my child to her. She showered me with gifts and tried to bribe me into giving my child to her. When I didn't, she suicided. Not long after that, I was given an air fare by the nephew of the owner of the club. He told me to go home. Had that not happened, I'm sure I would have got into drugs and prostitution.

I remember flying home with all my possessions and I cried all the way home and for weeks after. I never received any counselling. I just got pregnant again and had an abortion and it was only then that I went on the pill, which at the time seemed like a real sin, because I was raised a screwed-up Catholic.

Still I had no counselling and I drank heavily and chain-smoked to try to escape from my pain. I remember working behind a bar and one of my colleagues said to me that I had no expression in my face! Shortly after that, I just happened to mention that it was my birthday and when I was asked how old, he nearly flipped. I said I was twenty-one and he said, "What are you doing for your birthday?" and I said, "Nothing". So two gay guys and a manager took me out to dinner and made it a really good night, but, had they not said anything, the whole thing would have been 'business as usual'.

I don't recall ever being really loved at home. I became what was termed at the time as 'promiscuous', in search of love and affection. I thought at the time that it was the only thing I could do to get a hug, because I never got one at home. I don't remember any childhood birthdays, nor do I remember any happy times. It was just awful. Being the eldest, I was forever looking after my brothers and sisters while Mum was either sick, or in hospital having babies, while Dad was always drunk. The outings with Dad were always to the pub and he left us in stinking hot cars for hours, occasionally bringing out raspberry cordial to shut us up. Having said all that, I have had counselling and I think I have addressed those past issues.

Six years ago, I made contact with both my sons. Both reunions were good and we got along fine. I have met the adoptive parents and that went all right.

In 1973, I met my current partner, Allan and have been with him ever since. When we first met, things weren't really right. There was a lot of alcohol and a lot of the time life was a bit of a blur. I went from job to job, made lots of friends and partied, just to keep the past out of my head. He didn't want me to find my boys. He said that I gave up that right when I adopted them out and so I waited until they were in their thirties to contact them. Since finding my boys, I have felt a lot of relief and inner peace.

Two years ago, I went into rehab and got off the alcohol. Now we have a different relationship, because I am able to stand up for myself. Before, I would agree to anything, have a drink and didn't really care. Peter has been living with us for almost six years, less his stint in rehab for marijuana addiction. This took its toll on my relationship with Allan, because it was difficult to live with Peter when he was on drugs. Peter went into rehab for eighteen months and has been clean for three years. Now things are much better between Allan and him.

Up until March this year, Iann and I were in contact. I went to visit him in Adelaide many times and put in a real effort. He responded at the start, but now the relationship has fizzled out. He has major addiction problems and I have had to let him go.

I am now sixty years old and I work part time as a systems administrator. I have had a lot of ups and downs since I have been sober and I now realise why I drank. It was mainly to block out the adoptions and to put up with Allan. It is highly likely that we will separate soon. I'm still seeing my counsellor.

~~~~

Mireille's son was born in Australia in 1970

I lost my child to adoption, in 1970, in Sydney, after extreme pressure from my parents and society's values of that day. I was sixteen years old and my boyfriend was twenty. We were very much in love and wanted to keep our child, despite all the negativity that society placed on single mothers and fathers in the late 1960s. We asked my parents if we could marry, but that was flatly refused and because of our age we needed our parents' consent.

Then and now

Abortion was an avenue my father, who was a doctor, strongly wanted me to take, despite being five months' pregnant and the risk involved to both my unborn child and myself. He secretly tried to organise this and, upon hearing about it, I ran away from home for several days, before the police caught up with me and instructed me to return home. Nothing more was said about the impending birth. My boyfriend, who was made to feel very uncomfortable every time he visited, could not take the pressure and he left when I was seven and a half months' pregnant. He returned after two weeks and wanted to continue supporting me and be part of my life.

I was very distraught after my boyfriend left and my mother took me to a social worker, who suggested adoption. I had at that stage not even heard about it. She never offered any other alternative or even explained or explored what adoption meant. From that moment on the doctor who was looking after me put all the gears into motion. I remember her saying, "Oh, it's quite simple. We take the baby after birth and she can get on with her life. No one will know."

At delivery, I was told it was a boy and I screamed to hold him, but the nursing staff took him away and I was not to see him again for twenty-six years. They wheeled me into a ward where there were five other mothers and their babies. Because of my unrelenting crying they sent a hospital staff member (her role there I do not know to this day) who sat by my bed for a good hour, tersely telling me that I couldn't possibly change my mind, I must give up my son, how could I possibly raise this child on my own, I was too young, it was unfair to the baby and I was being very selfish, unreasonable and stupid. This was straight after the birth – I was exhausted, both mentally and physically and so I told her in no uncertain terms to leave me alone.

I spent approximately five days there and every time I tried to see my son in the nursery, staff would be there to take me back to the ward. All attempts were denied. The other mothers would breast-feed their babies and the curtains would be drawn around my bed whilst I cried constantly. Again, no counselling, no help…just negative vibes, punishment for being an unmarried mother. *Get on with your life and forget all about it* was the constant reinforcement made by everyone.

When the time came to sign the adoption papers, I was so exhausted, depressed and numb by the whole experience and lack of care by the hospital staff and society as a whole, that I signed the papers. There was only a representative from the Catholic Adoption Agency and myself present, no witnesses, no boyfriend (father to the child), just this lady and me. She was at least friendly and caring, but not much information was exchanged. *Just sign*. I remember being told something about thirty days, but I was too numb and exhausted to take in the information, crying throughout the whole procedure, which took about thirty minutes. The interrogation (that was how it felt) would at least cease and as they kept telling me that it was best for the baby, just get on with life and everything will be fine, I did what I was told. I now find out that my boyfriend, the father, could have been included on the birth certificate, something that was never discussed with me. To this date, his father's name is omitted on his original birth certificate. He was also denied access to his child, standing in the corridor whilst I gave birth but ignored and not spoken to.

At home, nobody talked about my recent trauma, just expected me to return to life as if I had gone in for an appendix operation. I was a walking zombie, depressed and not able to share my grief with anyone, including my boyfriend, who was afraid to mention the subject in case I got upset again. So I bottled it up deep inside, to surface frequently, sometimes resorting to looking at prams and babies about the same age, always hoping and wondering if he was all right. My boyfriend and I married two years after the adoption and had two more sons.

At the age of twenty-six, our adopted son made contact through the adoption agency. This is when the roller-coaster ride of emotions swept over me. So many things went around in my head. How would I tell my other two sons that they had an older brother; would they reject me and be angry? How would family and friends react? I needed help with the barrage of emotions ranging from euphoria to rage. Through the Sydney Adoption Agency, I was put in touch with ARMS (which, at that time, was called the Australian Relinquishing Mothers Society). What a relief it was to have such an organisation, which truly understood my dilemma, had untold information and, of course, the wonderful, gifted women who not only ran it but who shared the grief and truly understood. For the first time I realised that I was not alone.

My husband and I flew to Sydney six months later to meet our son and his fiancée. It was the most magical weekend of our life. We discovered that our son and his fiancée were getting married that year and that it was his wish for his two brothers to be his groomsmen. He was so happy that we had married and that he had two brothers. His wedding was tricky, but magic, with two sets of parents in the front row of the church and a parent table set up at the reception. They had really planned it so that we wouldn't feel left out – truly wonderful.

The downside of reunion for me was the nightmares, depression and, because of the unresolved grief, I really had to travel back in time and revisit being sixteen again, pregnant and all that came with it. I suffered Post Traumatic Stress and needed counselling throughout the entire time. Again, ARMS came to the rescue, as they had a professional counsellor who really understood all of these issues.

Many mothers, like me, felt that they were placed in a 'double bind' situation. Before signing adoption consent forms, they were told, *If you really love your baby, you will have him adopted* and afterwards the response became, *If you had really loved your baby, you would not have given him up.* This conspired to isolate relinquishing mothers and dissuade them from sharing their story – we had already been punished once for our misdeeds, why ask for more?

Our crime was that we were young and in love. Even though I was sixteen and he was twenty, in our eyes we were soul mates and we were happily married for thirty years, before I was widowed.

Our punishment was that we lost our first born child to adoption and subsequently three brothers lost out on their childhood together. There is a huge gap in our lives that will never be filled. We can only build towards the future and create that ourselves.

Our sentence? – Life! It is an experience that cannot be forgotten. I have forgiven and that has freed me. I don't want to become old and bitter. Nevertheless, I believe that someone should be made accountable for the actions that occurred in history, so that they are not repeated.

~~~~

Irene's son was born in Australia in 1971

In 1971 I was sixteen years old and became pregnant. I intuitively knew that I would give birth to a boy and I called him James, but did not tell anyone.

I gave birth to James who is now approaching the age of thirty-nine. He was given up for adoption shortly after his birth. I have learned that his adoptive parents did not keep this name. I have always referred to him as James.

I was born in Scotland in the mid 1950s. In the late1950s my parents, my younger sister and I migrated to South Australia where the family, except me, still remain. Our upbringing, joined by two brothers in the 1960s, was very tough. We attended Sunday school and church every weekend and had to pray daily.

When I was twelve years old my mother, my siblings and I converted to Catholicism.

Our strong religious convictions were also combined with corporal punishment for our shortcomings. This did seem to be the way of life during that time for many families. However, equating love with abuse contributed to some confusion, that took many years to come to terms with and heal from. Religious education in high school taught little if anything about adolescent body changes, how babies were conceived and certainly the word 'contraception' was not in the vocabulary. At least my mother did tell me how babies were made; I was very young at the time and I clearly remember not talking to my father for a week afterwards.

My mother lived with mental illness and was absent at various times throughout our childhood due to hospitalisation. My father worked three jobs to keep the family nourished. Being the eldest, I was responsible for my younger siblings. My sister and I did more than our fair share of household chores. We had rosters drawn up for the daily running of the house and everything had to be accomplished in addition to attending school and being expected to do well. Our younger brothers were a handful to say the least and often not manageable. I also remember being a very difficult and rebellious teenager. I left school at the age of fifteen and got a job as a nurse assistant in an aged care facility. A restrictive home life had taken its toll and I was longing to be let out of the 'prison' I felt confined in.

I had a friend at school who certainly had more freedom than I did and so I used to stay at her house at weekends. It was during this time that I met the person who would become the father of my baby. He and his friend had a car and so used to take us out to the drive-in movie theatre, as well as driving about to various places.

My boyfriend, who was four years older than I, was the only boy in our neighbourhood who had his own car. He would drive past my place to let me know he was in the area. That was my cue to take the family dog for a walk. Our poor family dog probably got walked more than any other dog in the neighbourhood.

I lost my virginity just before my sixteenth birthday. No prayer in the world was going to bring on my period and after a couple of months I had to accept the hard truth that I was pregnant. Oh no! What now? My parents were going to kill me! It turned out that they were all right once the initial shock of 'getting into trouble' was overcome. I was still living at home and I would probably have to give up my nursing job, as the work was demanding and heavy.

At the time I became pregnant my mother was ill again and I didn't want to add to her lack of wellness. It always seemed to be my fault whenever she 'broke down'. I went to Matron at the nursing home where I worked. She suggested that I confide in my mother's friend and she could help me tell my mother. Matron was caring and very kind to me. It was many years later after I was married and with my second born son that I saw her again at our local shopping centre. She was just as I remembered her and enquired about my life.

My mother's friend and I went home together to share the news with my mother, who was so upset that I didn't come to her in the first instance; she was furious! Meanwhile my boyfriend, who seemed to have vanished, ran off with my best friend and had no idea that I was pregnant.

I certainly wouldn't tell my parents who the father of my baby was. My father was ready to 'kill' whoever got me in this state. When my boyfriend did learn that I had become pregnant, he wasn't interested and pursued the relationship with my former friend.

I resigned from my nursing work, which I would return to after the birth of my baby. I continued to live at home until I was five months' pregnant. At that time my parents decided that I could not shame the family, as I was growing quite big with a pregnant belly. I went to reside at two different unmarried mothers homes.

I stayed at my first home away from home for the next three months. I lived with several other girls in the same predicament. We did chores and I remember working in the kitchen. I went into false labour in my eighth month, but no baby was forthcoming. I wasn't happy at this home, in part due to religious differences and secondly because girls had to feed their babies prior to giving them up for adoption. I thought that this practice was cruel. My parents allowed me to leave this residence and placed me at a subsequent one, where I was very happy during the last month of my pregnancy. Those in charge were very kind to us and I got on very well with the other girls. We mainly did laundry work, which I enjoyed. Some of us would sit up most of the night playing cards and I got quite good at playing 500.

My baby was due in December. No one had their baby on their due date. However, on the very day I was due, I started having contractions in the morning. They didn't seem too bad and so I didn't think much of it. By lunch time they started getting worse and it was decided that I get to the hospital. When our time came, one of the other girls would take us in a taxi to the designated hospital that was just fifteen minutes away. Our friend made sure we were safely handed over to the hospital staff. We would then be formally admitted and prepared for the delivery and our support person/s would be contacted. In my case it was my parents.

My parents could stay with me until the time for the delivery came. I didn't see them again until after I was settled into a ward. As soon as I delivered my baby, I was asked if my baby was to be given up for adoption. As I said yes, he was taken away from me straightaway. After the delivery I was placed in a six bed ward with five other post delivery women. The only difference was that they all had their babies rooming in with them. I can only assume that I had been put in that particular ward because of overcrowding, but I will never know.

As if that experience was not difficult enough, I had to endure the nasty attitudes from the nurse in charge. The loss of my baby, as well as the placement of me in this ward under these circumstances, caused me to go into shock and I remember being speechless and deeply traumatised by the whole event. The nurse in charge was insensitive and demanded to know what was wrong with me. I felt disregarded, disempowered, embarrassed and ashamed. I asked for the curtains to be placed around my bed. I was not even able to talk with my parents, when they came to visit me. It seemed many hours later when a young doctor came to see me. It was he who first showed me any comfort and compassion.

A social worker visited me the following day. She asked if I would like to go and see my baby. I was quite surprised that I could do this, but happy that I was able to. She took me downstairs to the new-born nursery area. As I looked in the window there seemed to be so many babies. The social worker arranged to have my baby's crib brought over to the window. On the top of his crib there was the name *James*. I asked her why the name James was on his crib.

She told me that all the babies in this section were waiting for adoption and instead of calling them babies *A, B, C* etc the nurses gave them names. She said my baby must have looked like a James. It was such an extraordinary thing because, as I said earlier, I never told anyone.

James was being tube fed which didn't look too good to me and so I was able to see him again before I left the hospital when he was able to suck and feed from the bottle successfully. The social worker asked if I wanted to hold him. It was painfully difficult for me to say no, but I knew I just couldn't. As was usual in those days I stayed in hospital for around eight to ten days before being discharged. No counselling was offered in those days and girls in my situation were advised to put it all behind us and move forward with life.

It was the week before Christmas when I returned home. It was not an easy Christmas for the family and has since been a very difficult time of year for me. James was not adopted until January 1972 and so, in comparison to us, he spent his first Christmas in hospital without his birth mother and subsequent adoptive parents. In January 1972 I signed the adoption papers and I tried to get on with my life.

I was still only sixteen years old, young and vulnerable. I was convinced that giving my baby up for adoption meant that he would be cared for in a loving home by a couple who probably couldn't have children of their own. I chose adoption for him with a Catholic couple mainly because I felt that he would receive a good education. Religious reasons were secondary, although I did feel at that time that it could provide a good start in life.

My mother wanted to adopt my baby and for me to be his sister. Given the traumatic childhood I had grown up in, there was no way that was going to happen. No other means of support was offered to me; I certainly didn't know of any that might have been available. I did what I felt was right at the time and in the best interests of my baby. To place my baby up for adoption was the most difficult decision I have ever had to make in my life and I have paid a huge price emotionally.

The pregnancy and birth of James has provided me with a significant key to my own personal psychology. I have been able to work through many issues which arose out of this event, within counselling and psychotherapy. I also choose not to work on James's birthday and spend this day in solitude and self care.

It is nearly thirty-nine years since his birth; our birthing experience. I still experience an intense time emotionally around that time of year. I have grown and healed as much as is possible. My healing is not complete, as James currently has a veto in place, which does not allow for reunion. My heart is open should he choose to contact me in the future.

My father now knows who my baby's father is. He says he 'always knew'. I never could keep anything from him. I have not had any further contact with James's father.

The relationship with my mother has always been a strained one, but in more recent times we are getting on well and keep in touch on a regular basis. We have never been able to speak of this event; one that I believe has greatly affected our relationship. All of my siblings know they have a nephew they have never met.

After a career in nursing and welfare practice I am now a counsellor with a special interest in grief and loss. I am still a deeply spiritual person, although the form that takes is very different from that of my childhood years.

The social attitudes in 1971 did not recognise that unmarried mothers had the same rights as married women. Our needs for the most part were profoundly overlooked and we were not cared for as well as we should have been. Social awareness has increased since then and attitudes have improved. However, for most of us, we continue to try to learn from the insights into our personal psychology which this experience has afforded us.

~~~~

Judith's daughter was born in Australia in 1973

These are the facts as I recall them and experienced them and, although I am not always clear on exact dates, they are, I believe, true and correct.

My mother took me to a doctor in a country town, when I was about four months' pregnant. He said that adoption was the only thing in a situation like this and that it was the right and best decision for both baby and mother. I sat in shock.

Then and now

No one ever asked me what I wanted, either during my pregnancy or after the birth. Adoption was never discussed with me. I was simply told that it was going to happen. The doctor had high praise for St Anne's Home for Unmarried Mothers, which was a Catholic home managed by the Sisters of Mercy. My Mum just agreed and so my parents in effect left me there. On my arrival a nun said to me that I should go and pray in the chapel for my sin ie having had sex outside of marriage. Even now, I find it almost unbelievable that, most days, I actually did do that.

About two weeks before my first child, a daughter, was born, I approached a nun and stated: *I do not want my baby adopted out*. I was lectured firmly and told that: *There are many deserving, infertile, married, Christian couples who have everything a baby could want and you have nothing. You can have a baby of your own when you get married*. I was even called selfish for ever thinking that I could raise my child. I do clearly remember this. My whole experience from the start was that I was to supply a deserving couple with my precious baby. Never did any nun refer to my baby as 'my' baby. I was told so many lies and I just believed them all. How could I have known any better then, being scared, vulnerable, alone and only sixteen years old?

I should have been able to see my baby and I did ask on three different days. I was denied each time. I was leaking milk from my breasts when I requested they take me to my baby. I was told again: *It's not your baby*. The nun told me to stay there and she came back with a binder, which she put tightly around my breasts and I was given tablets to dry up my milk.

I also believe that I was drugged so that I would not cause any problems for them, by asking to see my baby. The last time I asked to see my baby before leaving St Anne's, I was told yet again: *It's not your baby. You have your whole life in front of you. Just get on with your life and forget it.* The day my Dad came to take me home, I felt dead inside on leaving my precious baby behind. My first child was born on my seventeenth birthday.

Before falling pregnant and losing my baby, I was an everyday type of teenager, the happy-go-lucky type, although a bit shy and quiet, especially with males. After she was born I completed my training to be a nurse but then, about two to three years after her birth, I reverted to hiding myself in my parents' home. I was too scared to venture out because, even though I was no longer pregnant, I still felt the shame.

I would often go outside at night in my pyjamas looking everywhere under trees, bushes, even in our neighbour's garden, searching for my baby. I did this at least half a dozen times. One night my Dad come out and asked what I was doing. I said: *I'm looking for my baby. I know she's here somewhere.* My parents did not know what to do with me and took me to various mental health professionals. I was put on medication. I was eventually able to return to nursing, but attempted suicide about three years after the loss of my child.

When my daughter was about fifteen years old, I rang St Anne's Hospital. I spoke to a nun there and asked how my baby was. I was told that they had no current news, but they said that as a baby she was very happy and much loved by her parents. The nun said: *I'm concerned you are still upset after all this time and you have other children to cherish. Be assured that you made your decision and should learn to live with it.* I replied: *What decision? I never made one.* I was then told that in the days of the Bible I would have been stoned for having sex outside of marriage.

I did not know for fifteen years if she was dead or alive, but I never stopped trying to find out. In the end I hired someone to find her. My daughter and I are now in contact with each other and I am hopeful that our relationship will become closer over time. I have been speaking my truth of the abuse for some time. A friend and I appeared on the television programme, *The 7.30 Report*, over twenty years ago. But it seemed that the powers-that-be then were not ready to listen to us. Mostly I kept the secret of the fact that I had a baby out of wedlock to myself, apart from telling my husband before we were married.

It took me nearly thirty-five years finally to rid myself of my feelings of shame and guilt. Some things I have never forgotten and strangely, as the years have unfolded, I am remembering more and more of the abuse perpetrated on me. That is why I am now writing my story. I want justice for my younger self and for my first born; not just for me, but for everyone. This must never happen to anyone again, either here in Australia or overseas.

In 1973, I was told that, as a minor, I had no rights. I now know that this was a lie. I was denied my rights. Over the years I have said that my first born was taken from me for adoption. I have always said that I had no choice. As I have become stronger within myself, I have said that she was taken illegally from me.

Now I say that she was stolen from me, which, I believe, is closer to the truth. I very nearly lost my life because of the separation from my child. I was in so much pain and grief, although I did not realise then that it was grief. There is a lot more; these are only a few points. This is not about compensation. Even if I was offered all the money in the world, it could never make up for the loss of my daughter. I trust that truth and justice will finally prevail and at the very least I would like to receive a sincere apology.

[In response to this statement, Judith received a written apology from the Sisters of Mercy in 2010.]

~~~~

BJ's son was born in Australia in 1977

My strongest memory of being pregnant with my son, is a feeling that I had let and will continue to let everybody around me down. My life plan wasn't to be sixteen years old and pregnant.

I was a smart kid when it came to guys. I grew up in a Catholic family, went to a Catholic all girls boarding school and I was always considered to be one of the sensible girls – and I was. I was just unlucky to become pregnant.

The disappointment began with my mother. Just before I told my mother that I was pregnant, she was talking about yet another one of my friends who 'had to' get married. My mother, bless her, was quite a progressive lady in her time and most news that she received of a pending new life was greeted with, "Is she married?" You have to understand that I had two older sisters who 'had to' get married. One of them had already been through a messy divorce and my mother was now the primary daytime caregiver for my beautiful little niece.

Anyway, my mother and I were discussing the latest scandal, a friend of mine who 'had to' get married. I will always remember my mother saying, "If you get pregnant, I will knock your block off." What could I say? Being the straight-talking person that I am, "Well, Mum, you had better knock my block off, because I am." The next stage of this conversation was your typical tears from both Mum and me and words like, "You can say 'no', you know" (like it would make a difference now?) and, "Why haven't you got involved with a good Catholic boy?" etc. I don't think my Mum knew that there really was no such thing as a good Catholic boy, just boys and generally I did say 'no', but on this occasion, I didn't.

Of course, my mother told my father, who decided to have a conversation with his youngest child for the first time since she had last disappointed him. Well, they had eight children to raise and his job was to bring in the money. It was my mother's job to raise the children and deal with the teenage issues. That is how it was in the 60s and 70s. Anyway, another conversation I will always remember was the one he had with me. It was a bit one way, as you could imagine. His words, to this day, ring in my ears. "What a nice mess you have made of a young life" – and I had.

In fact, if I could have done anything to reverse the action and return to being that sensible, young sixteen year old girl, at this point, I would have done it.

During this time, my older sister was preparing to marry the man of her dreams and she had done me the honour of asking me to be her bridesmaid. She is still married to the man of her dreams, but, back in 1977, I was about to line up another person for disappointment.

She was hurt when informed that her head bridesmaid would be about eight months' pregnant by the time her happy day arrived. It took her a really long time to forgive me for spoiling her plans and even longer for me to forgive myself for the same.

When I said that the first person I disappointed was my mother, that was not quite right. There was someone else who knew before I told my mother. A young man whom I had begun seeing in recent months. He was a gentleman and, had I met him just a couple of months earlier, my life would have been different. Before we became a couple, we spent several evenings just talking and laughing and becoming really good friends. We both recognised something in each other that was going to lead to a much longer and stronger relationship than friendship.

Now, in 2010, we have been through an incredible thirty-two years of trials and triumphs. This has included twenty-six years of marriage, the incredible joy and sadness associated with raising three beautiful children, the devastating loss of paraplegia (him) and the stress and strain of divorce. Now, I think I can say that we have reverted to being friends again.

When I told him I was pregnant, he was devastated. He had finally met the woman he wanted to spend the rest of his life with and he was now confused as to what he felt for me. Was it love, was it care, was it pity, was it a need to protect me and fix the situation? He didn't know and nor did I. However, as our relationship became more solid, it became more obvious to me that I had to do the only thing I could do and that was do what I could to reverse the damage I had done to the people around me.

I had to relinquish the rights to this baby. I had to become the person I should have been. I told myself, right from the beginning, that I had no choice. This child could not be raised by me. How could I expect all of the people I had disappointed, to go on supporting me for the rest of my days, just because I had got myself into this predicament?

How could I expect my fifty-four year old mother to be the primary carer for my child, while I went to work and supported myself? This was 1977; there was no real support for teen mums like there is today. How could I expect my new boyfriend to marry me and raise a child who wasn't his? How could my father ever trust me to be the woman he had hoped I would be?

I met my relinquished son in 2006. We met because I had put his name into a website and he realised who I was. We had been sharing letters since he turned eighteen. In one of his letters, the department had forgotten to blank out his name and so I knew his full name for about ten years. I wanted to know what he looked like and where he was and all those things. We first started chatting through MSN. He told me I was going to be a grandmother soon. I received e-mails from his wife, who was excited about and supported the whole reunion and grandmother idea. She told me that I was welcome in their child's life and I could have whatever part I wanted in their lives.

We had a really lovely time getting to know each other and the only feeling I could compare the experience to was being in love. I was so excited about meeting my son for the first time. My husband supported me and was pleased for me.

We met soon after, on the 24th of March, 2006. After this, we continued to talk on the 'phone and through e-mail. My children all met my other son and his wife, on a few different occasions. I met his adoptive parents and they are lovely. His mother showed me a photo album that they had put together of him. When I opened the album and saw the photo of him as a baby, I began to cry. My son was out of the room at the time and his mother, who was sitting beside me, said, "Don't let him see you cry." I am not sure why she said that or why that was important to her, but I held back my grief and passed the album to my daughter, so that I didn't show my emotion. At about that time he came back into the room, probably just in time to see me pass on the album without looking at it.

My grandson was born in August, 2006. I was elated at the thought of seeing him and being a grandmother. However, he was born prematurely and very small and needed to stay in hospital for an extended time. I didn't visit straight away, as I wanted them to share his arrival with their families first. I visited for the first time when he was one month old. As I was spending that weekend nearby with my children, I called into the hospital on three different occasions.

On the last night I was in town I arrived quite late, about 6.45 pm. They had told me that they preferred not to have visitors past 7.00 pm and so I called to check it was still OK to come that late. I had arrangements to meet one of my children who was arriving home at 7.15 and so I was waiting out at the hospital, hoping to get a chance to see my son holding his tiny baby. As he was still quite fragile and in a humidicrib I didn't expect to hold him, but I did hope to see my son nurse him. At about 7.05, my son said to me, "I don't mean to be rude, but we don't like visitors after 7.00." Hospital visiting hours were until 8.00 and so I was hurt that I was just another visitor. I left very quickly. Since then, our relationship has been uncomfortable.

It was around about this time that my husband and I agreed that we didn't really have a future together. We separated in October, 2006. I reunited with my son's natural father for a short time. However, I realised that he was not for me. As it turned out, I was a lot wiser at sixteen than I was at forty-six. I am not sure how my son felt about that relationship. I now feel that I have somehow disappointed my son and my life has come around full circle. I know deep down that I have always done all I could do to be everything to everyone and made a selfless decision to 'fix' everything, then stayed in the background, waiting to be invited back into their lives. I realise that you can't fix everything. All you can do is what is right for you. I have always done what was right for everyone else, but I will never know if it has been the right thing for me.

I met up with my son a few years later and met my two beautiful grandchildren, now four and three years old. They were very excited and welcoming and proceeded to bring every toy out to show me. We sat on the couch and read books and they were such a delight. I hope to keep in touch with them and see them at least once per year. My other children are also keen to have an on-going relationship with their other brother and his family. So, fingers crossed our relationship will continue to develop.

~~~

Kim's daughter was born in Australia in 1984

When I was pregnant I played piano as much as possible so she would have music. I sang to her so she would remember my voice. I grieved her loss before she was born.

I felt her grow inside me and it went from feeling hijacked and scared to feeling protective and alone.

When I was pregnant I got a job but they fired me when they heard I was pregnant. I lived with my Dad and was lonely.

When I was pregnant I used to take the bus into the city and go into the shops that had beautiful prams and baby beds with lovely little blankets and cute mobiles to hang over the crib. I used to run my hands over the expensive furniture and wish that I could buy it.

When I was pregnant I learnt how to crochet with the other pregnant girls; a nun with facial hair and a kindly voice showed us. I made my child a blanket from pure wool. It took months to crochet. I had to wait for the money every two weeks to get more. Yes, I was that broke.

I also made her a patchwork quilt. I was trying to make her one like the ones in the shops. I chose that 'Liberty' material. It was very expensive and so I went to the *David Jones* department store every two weeks and bought strips of different materials. I was so bad at sewing it looked a mess when it was finished but I didn't know that. I saw the love that went into it.

When I was pregnant I didn't have any nice clothes to wear and so I sewed myself two maternity dresses. I had one pair of black maternity pants. I thought I was huge because I ended up weighing seventy-two kilos. If I weighed that now I'd feel thin.

My mother told me years later that I glowed and looked beautiful. I felt big and clumsy and ashamed like everyone was laughing at me for being pregnant.

When I was pregnant I slept with my hands on my belly and felt her move. I could see her move when I was in the bath. I could see her foot sticking out when she got really big. Was it her or me, but I craved coca cola like you'd never believe.

When I was pregnant I got a juice extractor and made healthy drinks. My belly got twice as big within weeks. I think it made her grow really fast. She was two weeks late. I rode my bike over bumps to encourage her to be born.

When I was pregnant I wasn't strong, even though I said, *No I don't want that*, the doctor let in five or six young male medical students and they all stuck their fingers inside me and practised. They had to because the doctor made them but they knew it upset me and they were not comfortable. I still get upset about that and feel violated.

ADOPTION SEPARATION

When I was pregnant I wanted to keep her and then felt she should be adopted, then wanted to keep her, but was brainwashed. I brainwashed myself. I believed that if you had a baby you couldn't go to university or travel. I was told that all the girls who kept their babies struggled and all the ones who relinquished flourished and did well.

When I was pregnant it was seen as something shameful and a big disaster. It was seen as something I had done wrong and as something that was an absolute tragedy. I was scared and confused and ashamed; none of those feelings you ought to have when having a baby.

When I was pregnant I thought that she would be better off with older people who had waited for years for a baby. I didn't think a girl who got pregnant when she wasn't supposed to was a good mother. I was told that these were good people; those poor people who waited and waited and waited for a baby.

I was brainwashed. I believed people who adopted were goodly and kind and honest.

When I was pregnant I told the people at the adoptions branch that there was no way I could do an adoption plan where you never hear any news; that it would kill me. They told me the people who were going to adopt her were more than willing to write to me once a year to give me news. I said I wanted her to be adopted by easy-going, flexible people. I just assumed they would love me as I loved them and want to know me later on in life and welcome me into their homes and hearts.

When she was just turned one the promise was broken. The yearly letters never happened and yes, it did almost kill me. I have never met them and am not sure how they feel about me.

When I was pregnant every time I talked about keeping her my mother would say something that undermined my confidence to be a parent. My baby's father left me, or I told him to go away because he was stressing me out. He wasn't nice to me. He was young and damaged and I'm not going to hate on him.

Then and now

When I was pregnant and almost ready to give birth I wrote her a letter. I so hate that letter now. I wish I had never written the stupid letter. It said awful things I think: stupid, ignorant, teenager, clueless about life things. I wrote it with my whole heart for her and wrote it with love but I feel like it says all the wrong things.

When I was pregnant I was her only mother. I wasn't a birth mother. I was her mother. When she was born she was so beautiful. I loved her so much it hurt. I secretly planned to take her home. I was too scared to say that I wanted to keep her.

I left her in the hospital and went and spent all my money on baby things, every single cent. Then there was no money left. I sat in my room at my Dad's house and panicked. I looked at the ugly toys that were there. Ugly second-hand plastic toys and a really awful doll that my Dad's girlfriend had given him for me. All these depressing, ugly, poverty things. I didn't know that those things didn't matter.

I went to the hospital to see her and held her in my arms. I was so confused and scared. The nurse there talked to me about how hard it was to raise a baby. While I had been in the hospital the social worker had told me I was taking the easy way out wanting to keep her. I telephoned my mother and said I was confused. I said I wanted to keep her and was confused and wasn't sure what I should do. I said I didn't know what to do.

She came in with her husband. She told me she was going to go with me the next day; we would sign the papers and I would go to Sydney. She bought me a one-way ticket.

The last time I saw my baby and I put her back into her plastic trolley bed she held on to my collar with her little hand. She held on to me and I put her down. God, that haunts me and if I could go back in time and hold on to my baby and have the courage to walk out of the hospital with her, then that's what I should have done. When I was in Sydney it was like walking in a dream. I was haunted. My sister said I looked disturbed. I cried every night and pined for my baby. I 'phoned my mother and said I wanted to come back and talk about it but she talked me out of it. I find it hard to forgive her for that.

When I was pregnant I was eighteen and scared and weak. My life has been changed in every way because of this one event in my life. It is with me every day. Thank God for reunion because the end of this hell has come but the shadow of it still haunts me. I run from it every day.

When I was pregnant I didn't know that I was beautiful. I didn't know that what was best for her was my voice, my songs, my piano playing and my body to keep her close and safe. I didn't have any trust. I didn't know that I was this amazing person.

When I was pregnant I was her only mother. Now I am the other mother.

Then and now

How it happened...

...in Canada

ADOPTION SEPARATION

Then and now

Lyn's son was born in Canada in 1963

It was very warm, that September, as she drove through dry, grassy slopes along the edges of the Okanagan valley. She was nervous and told herself to breathe deeply. When she did, she inhaled the sharp, sandy smell of the land. The smell of the earth brought her back from her fear and reminded her that she was alive; she could make her own choices now. Her choice, her work, had brought her to this moment. "He wants to meet me too," was her mantra.

Almost thirty years ago she heard her son's first cry and that was all the memory she had of him. They were separated immediately: the wisdom of the day. He stayed in the maternity ward until his adoptive parents came for him. She went on, trying to 'put it all behind her': another choice bit of '60s wisdom.

Who can ignore the longing for a child, or the constant awareness of something missing? There were the physical mementos of giving birth: the stretch marks, the swollen breasts, the slashed vagina. These would all fade, eventually. The dissonance of being a mother without the recognition, without the right to the name, without the right to the feelings: these were lasting wounds.

She thought about her son through the years: what he looked like, who his friends were, how his childhood went, but when she registered with the agency that would find him for her, she began to fantasize. The agency sent her 'non-identifying' information, as they called it and she learned that he was still in British Columbia. Every young male adoptee she met now held a new interest for her. She met a surprising number during that year of waiting. She felt that she was being readied.

Most of them were friendly enough, but there was an emotional reticence in all of them, which she later came to recognize as part of the psyche of the adopted child.

Her first shock, when the agency called to say they had located him, was his name. It wasn't the name she had given him. She had thought of him by that name all those years. Of course it wasn't the same name – all adoptees get new names, new birth certificates. She knew that, but it was still a shock. Reality slammed up against fantasy and fantasy fell back on its little, unreal behind.

Then they had their first telephone conversation. He told her not to be nervous, in a soothing, parental voice. He sounded nice and *old*. He was an adult. Of course – she knew that. She just didn't *know* it. For thirty years, he had been a baby to her.

She felt the weight of an iceberg of grief beginning to press against her. What they had missed! What they both had missed. He would have known that his new mother was not the one whose body had held him for nine months. He would have known by the smell. At least she had understood what she had done, even though she had as little choice as he.

She arrived at a friend's house and called him. He was soothing and calm; she was a wreck. They made plans for the next morning. It had been a long drive and she needed some rest and time before this ordeal. There seemed a million agonizing 'what ifs'. She hardly slept. Along with the anxiety and excitement, a mass of sorrow began to well up from her chest and lodge behind her eyes. She had been well trained in denial and so she hardly knew it was there.

As she got out of her car at his house, she could feel them watching her from the window. He opened the door before she could knock and she gazed into his unknown yet familiar face. He interrupted her staring by inviting her upstairs. She walked in a daze behind him to the living room, where he introduced her to his partner.

She sat on the couch and he asked if he should sit beside her. She wanted him to sit opposite her so that she could see him. His adoptive mother had prepared an album, sort of a 'this is his life'. She went through the motions of looking at the pictures, when all she wanted to do was look at him, let her eyes soak up all the looking she had missed. He was beautiful. Recognition came like the release of a long-held sigh. "Of course! Of course this is what you look like. Yes, of course!" All the fantasies disappeared the instant she recognized him. She didn't touch him that first time and realized later what she wanted was to hold him, to do what should have been done at the time of his birth.

The iceberg started melting on the drive home. She couldn't stop crying. She cried the whole eight hours to the throaty sounds of Bonnie Raitt belting out love songs, or the raunchy twang of the Indigo Girls bemoaning the wrongs of the world. The healing had begun. Rarely had she felt so alive. She had made her choice, met her son and as confusing and painful as it was, it was also the first crack in the shell she had built around her feelings. Her life would change quickly after this: she would found a support group, she would end a relationship, she would begin a new life. But for now, the smell of the earth, as she sped toward home, was rich and sweet.

~~~~

Peggy's daughter was born in Canada in 1968

Sometime in the fall of 1966, I was visiting my sister, Jane, in Toronto and she took me to the party of a friend of a friend, where I met a very nice looking Pakistani gentleman, who took a shine to me. I was nineteen years old and he was thirty-one. He pursued me rather aggressively and I was very flattered and so we started a long distance relationship.

ADOPTION SEPARATION

I was living in Ottawa in my parents' home. He would occasionally visit me on weekends and I would go to Toronto to rendezvous with him and stay with my sister.

On one such visit he was to get me to the airport to go home and he got me there late and I missed my flight. It was decided that we would go back to his place and he would take me to the airport the following day. We had never been intimate, but that was about to change. That night he took me into his bed and uttered the words, "I'll make a woman out of you" – that was the moment I got pregnant. This one act changed my status in society from an average middle-class twenty year old female to a wayward woman.

Denial took over and I started to count the days my period was late. When I got to ninety days, reality came crashing down on me. Life as I knew it was over. I called the father and told him I never wanted to see him again. What the hell was I going to do? Telling my parents was out of the question. Sex had never been discussed in our home and I couldn't stand the shame of telling them what had happened to me – not to mention the fact that my father would have killed me (or so I thought). They probably would have hidden me away in a Home for Unwed Mothers and I wanted nothing to do with that, because I knew they were horrible places.

As I explored my other options I realized there was only one and that was to run away. I got out a map of Ontario and identified the larger cities. Toronto was out, because that's where the father lived. The next largest city was London, Ontario which is about four hundred miles from Ottawa. A male friend of mine, Dave, the only person I had confided in, knew a couple, Paul and Martha, who had an apartment in London. He called them and asked if they could use some extra income and would like to take me in as a renter for the remainder of my pregnancy. They jumped at the chance and that became my escape plan.

Then and now

By now I'm almost five months' pregnant and definitely showing and so I went to a local department store to shop for a maternity outfit. I ran into a girl named Jennifer who had gone to the same high school as I did. We didn't like each other at all in school, but I felt OK greeting her and when she asked me what I was shopping for, for some unknown reason, I came right out and told her I was pregnant and shopping for a maternity outfit. Jennifer would become my lifeline.

Shortly thereafter at five and a half months and on a Thursday, I told my boss I was taking Friday off. On Friday morning I stayed in bed until I heard the front door slam twice, meaning both my parents had left for work. I got up and put on the maternity outfit I had hidden in the back of my closet. Then I placed an envelope containing a long letter to my parents, which gave them an explanation, but not my whereabouts. My friend, Dave, took me to the airport and I was off to my exile in London.

Paul, Martha and their toddler son met me at the airport and drove me to where I would call home for the next several months. Seems I wasn't renting a room but rather a shared space. They had a one bedroom, one bathroom, sparsely furnished apartment. I bought a black Naugahyde sofa to sleep on. This became the living room sofa. The back folded down and became my bed at night. It was kind of like the original futon only without the mattress and it was horribly uncomfortable. Although, as my stomach grew, it rested nicely in the crevice in the middle when I lay on my side. They never gave me my own key. Occasionally I would get a baby-sitting job that went a little late and when I came home they would be in bed and I was locked out.

There was also a single key to the mailboxes down the hall and I lived for my mail from Jennifer (during this period, I would receive a letter from Jennifer stating that she too was pregnant). Martha would make me wait for hours and hours to see if I had mail and, just because she could, she would decide to vacuum the living room early in the morning. She would vacuum all around and under me, putting an abrupt end to my slumber. The worst thing was that I did not have any privacy at all. There was nowhere I could go and shut the door, just be with myself, think and cry. However, on occasions when they all went out, I would sit with a cup of tea balanced on my belly and talk to my baby. I told my baby that it was he/she and me against the world. This is how it went until the day my water broke three weeks early. It was in April, 1968, on my twenty-first birthday.

Shortly after my arrival in London, I bought myself a plain gold band wedding ring. My public story was that my husband was in the military overseas. I also sought out the Children's Aid Society, because I thought they would give me counseling and support. Boy, was I wrong! They played on my vulnerability and shame and sapped me of what was left of my personal power, peace of mind and self-esteem. I was given no options whatsoever. I was told that I could not keep my child, over and over and over again. They said that keeping my baby would be selfish, whereas the unselfish thing to do would be to allow the child to go to a home where it would have a mother and father that could properly provide for it. I cried a lot and was labeled 'disturbed' – no kidding, who wouldn't be in my place? The more disturbed I got, the more unfit I was. Furthermore, I was told that, in time, after I got on with my life, I would forget entirely about this baby.

When my water broke I was told to go directly to the hospital, where my labor was induced. I was left alone in a very small, stark room that was barely larger than the bed I lay in. The pain of labor came as a horrible shock. I had not been given any coaching, education or printed literature concerning pregnancy and childbirth. Nor had I received any pre-natal (or subsequent post-natal) care and, in the absence of an advocate, I was left to deal with the pain without medication or consolation. Not being given anything for pain was a deliberate form of punishment for being bad.

I was in hard labor for almost two full days and then I gave birth to a beautiful baby girl, whom I named Kelly Grace.

Now the coercion to sign away all rights to my baby worsened. The hospital staff and my social worker considered me uncooperative, because I would not sign the papers they wanted me to sign. I was told that I could not leave the hospital with Kelly Grace. On the day I was discharged I stood at the nursery room window for what seemed hours, until someone told me I had to leave. Before I left London to return to Ottawa, I asked to go to court to request three months' temporary wardship for Kelly, to buy some time in the hopes that my parents would help me keep her or I could come up with some way of making it on my own. I was also holding out hope that, once Jennifer's baby was born, we could both keep our babies and raise them together. What I did not know was that going to court meant that I had already given up most of my rights and, after the three months, I would have to prove to the court that I could provide for my child.

I returned to my parents' home and a newly decorated bedroom – I suppose this was to signify a new start and the beginning of my forgetting that I had a baby. It didn't work. My friend, Jennifer, was now at the stage where she needed to be hidden away and so my parents offered to take her in for the balance of her pregnancy. She slept in the other twin bed in my room.

My Mom and Dad were wonderful to her, which made me wonder why they weren't wonderful to me. My baby was not talked about at all. At no time was I asked how I felt. Everyone acted like nothing had happened, while I was dying a slow and painful emotional death. My three months went by quickly and I was summoned to return to court in London.

My mother held the front door open as I exited the house to catch a train to London. She asked me what I was going to do and I answered, "I can't give up my baby". I arrived in London a day early, because I demanded to see my daughter, totally against the advice of my so-called social worker. I was put in a little room with just a table and a chair. Kelly was brought to me and I was told I had one hour. She was three months old now and I was shocked at how much she had grown. I walked in circles around the room holding her and crying. I could tell she remembered me – she did not fuss or cry the entire hour.

I undressed her and dressed her, trying to pack a lifetime of mothering into one hour. I had knitted her a pair of bootees (the only thing I had ever knitted in my life) and I tried to put them on her, but they were much too small – this, too, was heartbreaking. Our hour flew by. I handed my daughter back and would not see her again for twenty-six years.

I arrived at the Court House, a total wreck, the following day. My social worker gave me some kind of sedative in pill form – was that even legal? I was put on the stand and the Judge asked me what plans I had made for my baby. I burst into tears and my social worker began talking for me. The next thing I knew was the Judge's gavel slamming down, declaring Kelly Grace a Ward of the Crown. I don't remember signing anything. I was completely dazed. I died that day. Why did I have to go through this alone? I have a family – why didn't someone insist on being there for/with me?

I didn't know where to go and I had nowhere to go – no car, of course and so I just wandered off. When I came upon a movie theatre I went in and watched a movie (*The Thomas Crown Affair*) that I didn't really see at all. The sun was still high in the sky when I exited the movie theatre and I thought, "Will this day never end?" I resumed my wandering and came across a closed bar. I read the sign on the door with their hours of operation. Since the bar would be opening in about an hour, I decided to sit on the curb and wait. I was barely drinking age. I had just turned twenty-one before my daughter was born. When the door opened I went in, sat down and started drinking.

I vaguely remember guys coming and going, asking me if they could join me and engaging in meaningless bar talk. I was still there for last call. I closed the bar and walked out into the street, cold sober. All night I had been pouring alcohol into an empty vessel and I couldn't even get drunk.

A few months later, I received a letter from the Children's Aid Society stating that my daughter had been adopted. Up until then I still thought of Kelly Grace as being mine – but she was gone forever now. Shortly thereafter, I took a massive overdose of pain killers, which I had carried in my purse throughout my pregnancy, just in case things got to where I could no longer stand it. I had a picture of Kelly protected in plastic and had written, "I love you" in lipstick across it.

It was about 3:00 am and I had ingested about three-quarters of the bottle when I went to the bathroom to get more water to take the rest of the pills. I passed out and my mother heard me hit the floor from downstairs. I was rushed by ambulance to emergency, where my stomach was pumped. They saved my life, but within a few weeks I discovered that the overdose had damaged my kidneys and for the next four years I was either an inpatient or an outpatient and considered to be potentially terminally ill.

Today's science understands the chemical changes that occur with pregnancy and childbirth and women are routinely treated for what is now referred to as postpartum depression.

If that was all I had to deal with, it would have been at least tolerable. However the enduring damage that was done was due to the secrecy, lack of acknowledgement, counseling and support, abandonment issues, self loathing, shame, guilt, loss of self-esteem and self-confidence and the constant wondering if my baby was well and happy or being abused.

Additionally, there is a misconception that reunion fixes everything and rights the wrong. The truth of the matter is that reunion brings up a whole other Pandora's Box concerning all the lost years. I never did get my baby back – I got back an adult stranger. I am sixteen years post-reunion now and it is still hard to integrate the beautiful, intelligent, totally delightful woman that has my DNA with the precious baby that was taken from me.

My life has not gone as intended. This pregnancy changed its course. Like approximately thirty per cent of all birthmothers, I never had another child. I have been diagnosed with chronic depression and post traumatic stress disorder. I have married and divorced three times and been institutionalized for extreme depression three times.

I have never been one to wallow in my loss. Quite the contrary, as I am considered to be a very high energy, 'up' person, but the fact is that severe damage was done when an agency, the Government, the medical community and society at large took my child and beat me to a pulp while doing it. I was not allowed to mourn and that damaged my soul. It made me different and darker than most people.

I am sixty-three years old now and I have learned many lessons. One such lesson is that I am best off living alone. I live in Southern California with all my family still in Canada. I bask in the knowledge that I have a forty-two year old daughter, Miranda, a sixteen year old grandson and a thirteen year old granddaughter in my life. I feel that I am at the top of my game. Life can't hurt me anymore. I am a survivor.

~~~~

Jennifer's son was born in Canada in 1968

When I was nineteen years old, vulnerable and with no established boundaries, my new-born son was taken from me and given to a married couple, who adopted him and raised him as their own. It was 1968 and I was not married. In those days, this was the normal and acceptable treatment for 'unwed mothers'.

We had sinned and brought shame on our families. As a result, society judged us unfit to be mothers. We were stigmatized and shame was heaped upon us. We bore this shame alone – the term 'unwed fathers' did not exist.

The social worker at the Children's Aid Society told me that it was not acceptable to raise a child without a father. My child would be illegitimate or, in cruder terms, a bastard – a stigma that would follow him for the rest of his life. I was counselled to put him up for adoption. If I loved my child, I would give him to a married couple. No other options were ever discussed.

During the last months of my pregnancy when the shame was becoming visible, I had to go into hiding. I stayed with the parents of my friend, Peggy. She was also an 'unwed mother'. Her daughter was now three months old and in a foster home. She had not signed the relinquishment papers, as she hoped that we could keep our babies and raise them together. That summer I lived in a protected bubble. That bubble burst when my water broke.

At the hospital, I was left to go through labour alone. After many hours with no comforting voice or presence to anchor me to reality, I became delirious. I was wracked with pain and shivering uncontrollably. The nurses told me that I was making too much noise and disturbing the other mothers. When the doctor finally arrived, I was anesthetized. I thought I was being suffocated and fought as the mask covered my face.

When I regained consciousness, I felt as if I'd been washed up on an alien shore, shipwrecked and alone. The social worker from the Children's Aid Society soon arrived at my bedside with the forms to relinquish my new-born baby. She told me that I'd had a blonde-haired, blue-eyed boy – a 'blue-ribbon baby'. She urged me to sign the forms so my son could go to his new home as soon as possible. She returned every day, but I didn't sign the forms.

ADOPTION SEPARATION

I was intensely lonely during my stay in hospital and that loneliness has never really left me. I shared a room with a married woman whose baby was brought to her for feeding. Her side of the room overflowed with visitors and flowers. I was isolated behind a curtain. I sat alone on my bed, my chest tightly and painfully bound to stop my milk from coming in. Down the hall, my son lay alone in the back row of the nursery. When I went to the nursery to look at him through the window, the nurses ignored me and didn't move him closer.

I know now that the Children's Aid and hospital staff had no legal right to keep my son from me. I hadn't signed any forms yet. I could have left the hospital with him, but I didn't know that. The truth was that I had nowhere to take my son. I knew all along that I couldn't keep him without my parents' support. My parents, however, didn't want anything to do with me until 'the baby' was gone. They didn't want to know what he looked like or where he went. They were concerned with what people would think, not with the well-being of their daughter and first grandchild. We never discussed the loss of my baby. His absence separated me emotionally from my parents for the rest of our lives.

Without my parents' support or any counselling or information about how I could raise him on my own, I signed the forms relinquishing my son when he was two months old. My only other contact with the Children's Aid was a letter informing me that my son had been adopted and a brief paragraph describing his new family. This non-identifying information was all I was entitled to. I never heard from them again. They had what they wanted.

When my son was adopted, a new birth certificate was issued in the name of his adoptive parents. I had carried him inside me for nine months and given birth to him, but it was as if I never existed. The records were 'sealed' to make sure that the shameful secret of his birth didn't somehow leak out.

Then and now

He was born in early September and so I was able to return to university and complete my final year without anyone knowing what had happened.

I was denied the right to be a mother to my son and I was also denied the right to grieve his loss. Despite the assurances of the social workers at the Children's Aid that I would forget him, I spent the next thirty-three years living with my unacknowledged grief. I was deeply wounded and suppressed my feelings of anger and sorrow. I suffered recurring anxiety and depression. I had a series of unhappy relationships and I never married. I was steeped in shame. I had a deeply-rooted feeling that I was not good enough. I concealed this, however and mastered the art of 'looking good'.

At thirty-eight, I gave birth to a beautiful baby girl. Although her father left soon after her birth, I was in a very different place than when I had my son. I owned my own home and had a secure job. I was able to bring my daughter home and raise her on my own. When my daughter was two, I went back to the Children's Aid Society to find out what I could about my son. Even though he was now an adult, I was still not entitled to any information. Feeling hopeless and defeated, I suppressed my pain once again.

My daughter was a blessing and gave my life meaning. Having another child, however, did not replace the one I had lost. For all those years, I didn't know my son's name or even whether he was alive. I wondered if he knew he was adopted and if he thought about me and why I had abandoned him. I felt profound guilt and sorrow. I now know that my son's name is Andrew. When I finally met him again, I recognized our connection stamped on his face and shining in his eyes. I finally got to hold my son when he was thirty-three years old. But the baby I lost is now a tall, handsome man, sensitive and articulate. There is no way to get back all the lost years.

There's a tendency to think of reunion as a happy ending. While it's a profoundly joyful and momentous event, it's far more complex than that. Reunion is a turning point in the lives of those involved. It brings a release of emotion and a journey into uncharted territory. When I reconnected with my son, along with the joy came all the pain and unresolved grief. I came face to face with the immensity of my loss. I've had to deal with my issues of loss and betrayal and not burden Andrew with my pain. I have struggled to find my place in his life.

Reformed adoption legislation is slowly opening up birth and adoption records that were sealed long ago. The adoption laws were finally changed in the province of Ontario in 2009. Most of us who lost our children to adoption and our now grown children can apply for and receive each other's names. It has taken many decades and is only happening because groups of birth parents and adoptees, such as Parent Finders of Canada, are lobbying for it. Adoption records are still closed in some provinces of Canada and in many states in the U.S.

I feel that adoption fails to balance the rights and interests of birth parents, adoptive parents and adoptees. The adoptive parents have always been the first priority. In the past, most adoptive parents were told that the babies available for adoption were unwanted and needed a home. Our 'unwanted babies' provided a convenient solution to married couples, who could not have children of their own. Their desperate desire to have children overshadowed the pain caused by separating these children from their mothers.

For many years, I tried to believe that it was best to give my son up for adoption. But today, I can no longer believe that it was best for me; or that it was best not to tell the truth about what happened and to deny my son the right to know the true story of his own history and his family of origin. There is nothing so terrible about the truth that it must be hidden behind secrets and denial. Adoption can bring great happiness to adoptive parents, but leaves pain and anguish in its wake.

The secrecy and lies that have always surrounded adoption are very difficult to dispel. We mothers who lost our children to adoption are finally joining forces and speaking our truth. It is time for governments to acknowledge past mistakes and apologize to birth parents and adult adoptees for the harsh and unfair way we were treated.

Only then can we move forward and make informed and compassionate decisions that will respect the rights of all involved. We need to ensure that separating babies from their mothers is a last resort, taken only after all other options have been explored. If adoption is the best and only option, then we need to make sure that people will no longer be denied the truth about who they are and where they come from.

~~~~

Sandra's son was born in Canada in 1969

It began again with my youngest sister, who decorated in black and gargoyles, asking me to go to her bedroom to discuss decorating tips. Unlikely... But, when I asked her what was wrong and assured her she could ask me anything, she blurted out, "It's not about me; it's about you!"

I was found. My son had found me through her, in the one week her telephone number was available to him. He had also found me and left me a message, but I was out West dealing with my father's death and had not yet heard it. I knew my life would change; I did not know how or how much.

When I was sixteen, I had become pregnant and my son was born the day before I turned seventeen. His father supported me during the pregnancy, but did not see himself raising his son with me. In the late sixties, when he was born, it was not easy to keep one's child when young and single, without family support. There was already a large demand for adoptable (healthy, white, new-born) children. Without a clear idea of how I could support myself, much less my child, I lost him to adoption.

I knew to be careful of a couple of things: he was healthy, I was told and the social worker assured me that he would not be more than a week or ten days in foster care. He must not languish in foster care, I thought. That was my fear, having been in foster care myself. Even at seventeen, I could do better than that.

Losing my son made me not interested in young children. I coped by never thinking of him, as much as I could manage that. My husband married me knowing that we would never have children. Though I worked in schools, it was at the high school level. No little children for me!

At one point, fifteen years later, I was made to work with younger children, six year olds, as part of my educational program. I discovered I liked them. As I neared twenty years after the birth of my son and eleven years with my husband, I finally felt enough trust (and knew now that I earned enough even on my own) to have another child. It was actually a little traumatic to have another child. How can one act as though this is the first and not the second child? How could I not fear losing this child in some way also? Could I trust this man to stay and love his child?

Now, when my second child was nine years old, here was her older, much older, brother to explain to her. Here was I, with some status in a small town, having to acknowledge having been a 'loose' girl in my youth. Here was my son.

I have said that the loss of my son, denied for twenty-six years, accrued interest in the passing years. I don't know if open adoption would have been easier for me; I do know that it was awful to thaw the frozen core of me that was his loss. I cried for days, even years. This was mixed with the glorious joy of knowing him again and rejoicing in his wish to be connected with me and his natural family. It was a crazy-making process, mixing the joy and sorrow and so confusing.

I've heard it said that many natural mothers, upon reunion, remake their lives, changing husbands, jobs or where they live. There was a short time when I found making decisions impossible. Me, the most decisive of people! How could I know upon what basis to make any decision? I was re-thinking the biggest decision I thought I had ever made, in losing my son. How much choice had I really had?

I had no preparation for his return. I had a lot to learn. My son had prepared himself and that helped to some degree. It turns out that he was very much like me. Some children are half of each parent, but not this son. He was about eighty per cent me and only a little like his father. So, finding me, he snapped to the template.

I have come to believe that raised children often see their parents' tendencies and how those turn out and so they decide to be different. My daughter, knowing that I was interested in biology, decided she would be different and took physics. She wanted to be her own person. Those lost to adoption, though, never see where their natural traits lead and so they run down the track laid out by nature. Thus it was with Glenn; he and I had so many similarities it was eerie. It fuelled our relationship in the early years, because it seemed so easy and natural.

It soon became apparent, however, that this business of putting a child into another person's home is a lot like leaving a cuckoo's egg in another bird's nest. The fit is bad. So it was with Glenn. His adoptive parents were not bad people and they loved him as they knew how, but it was a spectacularly bad fit temperamentally for him. They did not understand him and did really a poor job trying to raise him. The scars of that will remain with him all his life.

Between Glenn and me and the Freedom of Information Act, I found that, added to the trauma of losing his mother at birth, he went through two foster homes in those first months. He did not get to his adoptive home as I was promised until about four months had passed. Thus, what I was most afraid of turned out to be what happened.

I felt betrayed. The social worker, in her inexperience or incompetence, had not correctly completed the paperwork and so at about the month and a half mark, when he was being moved from his first to his second foster placement, I was called back to sign the papers again. I went to the social work office intending to get my son back. Somehow and to this day I don't know how, I came out of the office with the papers signed again and without my son. Since he had not been adopted when I was called to re-sign the papers, why was I not told he was still not adopted?

That social worker knew how I worried about that. I was still legally his mother at that point. Had I no right to know what was happening to my son? Where were her professional ethics? It could not be argued he'd bonded with his foster or adoptive mother. They were moving him anyway and his 'forever' family did not exist in any fashion at that point.

Furthermore, I wrote and asked at the one year mark whether his adoption had been finalized. In my naïveté, I thought that, perhaps, if the placement were not finalized, I could get him back. I did not hear back for a while and was finally sent a letter saying he was in a permanent placement. With more experience and with all the paperwork obtained through the Freedom of Information legislation, it is clear that his adoption could not be finalized at the one year mark, because he had not been placed until he was about four months old and that this adoption was rushed through at the point of my letter requesting information. This does not seem to reflect honesty in the process. The information to me as mother was incomplete at best and deceptive at worst.

In coming to know my son in the first years after we re-connected, three things were clear to me. First, that he was wonderful, bright, engaged, compassionate and with broad interests. Second, he had been poorly mothered, which affected his basic sense of self and ability to form loving relationships. Third, he had huge loyalty issues conflicting with his desire for independence as a young man. How do you re-parent an adult, to provide the basic sense of trust impaired by his losses and upbringing?

I used to say that he called the mothering out of me. He enjoyed and wanted things any child wants from his mother: my attention, even at two in the morning if that's when he needed me. He needed to know he was adored and he revelled in that. He felt that things were orderly and clear around me, rather than confusing as they were in his adoptive family. However, he could not acknowledge me as mother, because to do that was to take from his adoptive mother and in some way that scared him terribly. My daughter was unquestionably his sister, but I could not be called his mother.

Difficulties existed as we made our way in reunion, some from my son and some from me. Our strength was our commitment to communication: we always talked and our talking and writing to one another helped us work through many issues.

I took time to connect my nine year old daughter with her twenty-six year old brother. It turns out that playing video games is something that can engage both ages. As he taught her to play the games, they forged a strong bond. The two of them are now close. I helped Glenn find his father and they connected, but have little enough in common that they are not close.

I have seen with many sons lost to adoption three patterns for forming relationships. Some young men choose a partner young and stick with that partner, for good or ill. This turns out well if the choice is lucky and poorly if the choice is not. Another pattern is serial monogamy, one relationship after another, with the son often leaving the relationship before he is abandoned again. A third pattern is never settling into a relationship. I find that many sons lost to adoption struggle in their romantic relationships, more collateral damage of adoption. This is never counted in the ledger of adoption, when it is argued how successful adoption is as an institution.

At about the eight year mark into our relationship, we were again trying to explore what it meant to be family. Glenn suggested I try treating him as 'just a friend,' instead of family. Something broke in me at that suggestion. I began immediately to treat him as I would a friend, rather than my son. After about eighteen hours of that, he said, "I don't like this. I want to be family." It was hard for me, though. I could not imagine losing him again, which was what 'being friends' entailed and having had to imagine it, I found it hard to trust 'being family' again. The pain in losing him again was still too close to the surface.

This time in our relationship allowed me to step back slightly and protect my emotional self a bit from Glenn's difficulty relating to me as his mother. I still think of this as a very difficult time.

In the years to come, as my son went through good times and dark times, we have remained close. At one point, denied permission to move back into his adoptive mother's home after the loss of his adoptive father, he turned to me and now lives in a suite in our house, far from his adoptive family.

Fifteen years into reunion, I have a wonderful, loving son, who lives close to us and is connected and involved in the life of our family. He and I and my husband have found a way to live in harmony (most days!). This past summer, I fulfilled a lifelong dream by travelling to places I have always longed to see with my two children. It was a pure joy to have them both with me and to have unsullied time with them both. The two of them are closely connected and enjoy one another so much.

I worry that Glenn sees my strength and close connection to him in the same mould as the need to control that he experienced growing up from his adoptive mother.

Then and now

We each bring who we are into reunion, but we cannot determine how that is perceived by the other party.

In adoption, we all have control issues. As mothers, we had no control when we lost our children and so we have issues around control ever after. Many children who were adopted also feel a lack of control, as they had no say in being transferred from their families to strangers in the adoption process and so many adoptive parents, foiled in their control over their own bodies, unable to have their own children, feel it necessary to control the children they acquire, lest these children return to their natural families, in affection or in fact.

Even more so for the natural mothers, who, having lost their first child to adoption, experience secondary infertility and go on to adopt someone else's child. How difficult it must be to live inside their heads, with the knowledge of what it's like to lose a child, yet also having taken one from another mother.

With a reasonable amount of contact in reunion, it's often at about the three year mark when one begins to see how it will go. Sometimes, stalled or denied reunions re-kindle after a decade or more, often when there is a change in the life circumstances of son/daughter or mother. Glenn and I know we'll be close. I don't know what he will do with his life and I am not sure he does either. I do know he'll be OK and a part of being OK is being close to me, his step-father and his sister. I do know that my life is enriched through him having found me, despite the dark thread that his loss will always be in the tapestry of my life.

ADOPTION SEPARATION

How it happened...

...in England

ADOPTION SEPARATION

Then and now

Sheila's son was born in England in 1958

At the age of seventeen, after a brief affair, I became pregnant whilst training to be a nurse.

It was 1957 and I was living in Yorkshire. As the pregnancy was not confirmed until four months, termination was not a possibility. Abortion was illegal at the time; however termination was available illegally, in some private clinics, if funds were available. There were also back-street abortions, which were potentially very dangerous to pregnant women and their babies. I was aware that I did not have a partner to share the situation and did not have any idea what to do next.

I informed my parents, who, like myself, were in a state of shock and disbelief. My mother was concerned about me and the future, but my father was angry and rejecting. I had brought shame on the family and "never darken my doorstep again" was his reaction. If I had decided at that moment that I wanted to keep the baby, my mother would have left my father to support me. As I had a seven year old brother, I could not let her split the family for me. I was not allowed to return home in the foreseeable future.

The local Vicar was contacted and put me in touch with the Church Adoption Society. Subsequently, I was summoned by the Matron of my Hospital, given my notice and informed that I could not continue my training.

For the next few months, I went to stay with my grandmother, in a city twenty-four miles from my home, to prevent anyone there from knowing about my condition. Although anxious about the future, I was treated kindly, non-judgmentally and sympathetically by my Gran and her friends. As she lived in a one roomed flat, I could not stay there permanently.

ADOPTION SEPARATION

When I was seven months' pregnant, I was allowed to go to a Mother and Baby Home in the West Riding of Yorkshire. This was an old Victorian house, like a small workhouse and reminded me of a milder edition of Dickens' Dotheboys Hall. There was plenty of hard work, as there were about twenty girls and babies looking after themselves, with a Matron and assistant in charge. We were expected to be sorry for our actions and grateful for a roof over our heads. The youngest girl there was twelve, but was still expected to look after her baby in the nursery as necessary.

Throughout the previous seven months, no one had mentioned the possibility of keeping my child with me, adoption being the only option proposed. I was also aware that I could not support myself and a baby, with no job, child care, or accommodation.

Towards the end of my pregnancy, there was an influenza epidemic at the Home and I went into labour after contracting the disease. My son was born in the local hospital and the experience was frightening, not helped by the rough treatment by the delivery doctor and condemning attitude of some of the staff. The other mothers in the ward were kinder and more understanding of my situation, but the hospital stay felt like a punishment for having a baby 'out of wedlock'.

We were expected to breastfeed our babies at the Home, as well as all the other care necessary, learning from each other. As the babies were in one dormitory, we had a rota for night duty and, if it was our turn, we were responsible for ensuring that, when a baby cried, the mother was contacted to see to its needs.

Shortly after my discharge from hospital, I was visited by the Adoption Society social worker, who treated me with respect and compassion. She explained the adoption process and I accepted that this was the only viable option for me and in the best interests of my baby, in order for him to grow up in a loving family environment.

Then and now

Subsequently, I was informed that prospective adopters had been found and would be visiting the Home to see the baby. I was not allowed any details other than that they were teachers and happily married.

I left the Home after about six weeks and, accompanied by the social worker and my baby, went to the Adoption Society offices in York and handed him to the social worker, who took him to another room where the adoptive parents were. Although I kissed him goodbye and held on to his shawl, as they had another for him, it seemed an unreal happening and emotionally I did not feel I was saying goodbye to him forever. I did not have a photograph of him or any other memento.

I returned to my parental home, as my father allowed me back without my baby, as no one in the town knew what had happened. My career in nursing was resumed at another hospital, although I was very unhappy and felt a big hole in my life.

A few months afterwards, I was contacted by the social worker. When she visited, I was in bed, sleeping following a night shift. She brought me papers to sign which finalised the adoption.

It was not possible to find out any further information, but when the contact register was established, I put my name on it, hoping that it might result in further knowledge about my son.

Meanwhile I had married and had two children. My husband was aware of my earlier history, but I did not tell my children until they were settled with their own families. I have not shared my 'secret' with my present friends and colleagues, as it is a very personal one and I do not want to cope with their reactions, however sympathetic they may be.

When it was legally possible, I traced my son via a registered agency and, although he had decided not to try to contact me, we have exchanged letters. I have learned that he had a very happy, fulfilled child and adulthood with his loving adoptive parents.

I could not have given him this and so, although I have had to live with the pain and loss of a child, it has become less intense over the years.

I feel very privileged that I have had the opportunity to know that in the circumstances existing in the 1950s, I gave my child the best start possible in his life by having him adopted.

~~~

Anna's daughter was born in England in 1960

"You have a little girl!" my charming, Indian doctor told me and I cried with joy and relief, just before the anaesthetist knocked me out. It was a breech delivery, but the doctor knew I wanted to know the gender of my child before the head was delivered. I had been told throughout my pregnancy that girls were easier to get adopted than boys and so I had hoped and prayed that I would have a daughter. My wish had been granted. My illegitimate child would have a home and parents. I did have a little fear, nonetheless, for my child was not a pure Anglo-Saxon. Her father was English but I was of Mediterranean descent and my daughter's mixed blood could be a disadvantage when it came to having her adopted.

Why had I decided that my baby would be adopted? I was training as a nursery nurse, working with children from broken homes. The advantages of adoption were always extolled. We had heard many lectures on the subject and it was clear that adoption was the best chance an illegitimate child could have. As soon as my pregnancy was confirmed, therefore, I decided on adoption for my child and when I wrote to my father, who was a barrister, to give him my news, I told him that I was pregnant and that the child was going to be adopted, all in the same sentence.

Then and now

He welcomed me home and a long series of lies began. My Roman Catholic Mother was heartbroken because I had 'sinned' and it was important to her that as few people as possible knew the truth. I was not able to stay at home for long, although my father was kind and supportive, in case anyone else realised my condition. I soon returned to London to work in a department store and lodged with some friends of the family.

While I was at home, I tried to explain to my sister how the pregnancy had come about, although at the time I did not realise that I had actually been raped. I had always associated rape with screams and violence. I had been too shocked to scream and so I took the guilt upon myself, blaming myself for having allowed it to happen. I was on a double date with my friend and she and her date were just around the corner in a dark alleyway when it happened. The young man I was with was known to me, as his brother had been my boyfriend for a little while. He was not very violent, just very strong. He held my wrists behind my back and when I realised what he was going to do I tried to kick him in the groin. This made him nastier and rougher. He hit me in the face and the whole thing was over in a few minutes. I felt ashamed and horrified and thought straight away that I could be pregnant. However, after talking to my friend, I started to think it was less likely. I was so naïve that I thought I wouldn't get pregnant if I hadn't enjoyed it! As soon as I returned to the nursery I had a hot bath.

I met the father again once only, by chance and told him I was pregnant. He flew into a rage. I managed to escape from him and feared meeting him again for many years to come. At least I was spared one heartache that many unmarried mothers had to face – I wasn't deserted, for I never loved or cared about my child's father. I only hoped that my child would not grieve for her unknown father. I met another boyfriend, who supported me through the pregnancy and who is still a friend. I don't know what

I would have done without him. He wrote to me frequently from where he was studying in Dublin.

I gave up my job when I was about six months' pregnant. My parents and I visited the Adoption Society and one of the colourless, stern officials there outlined the plans, talking about me as if I wasn't there. She gave us the address of the Mother and Baby Home I would attend. I was afraid that it was in the same area where the brother of the father of my child lived and I was terrified of meeting him again, but my fears were dismissed. It was all arranged. My mother was just happy that it was a Catholic agency. Then I had a lovely holiday with my parents, during which I wore a wedding ring, as was my mother's wish. I removed it when she'd gone. Before going into the Home, I spent some time in a beautiful Cathedral town. I was sustained by my friend's regular letters from Dublin. During my time at the Home I wrote fantastic letters to my aunts and grandmother about the great jobs I had in London and all the great parties I was going to!

In my time at the Home, I built relationships with the other young mothers there. We comforted and consoled each other. There were eleven or twelve of us and three nuns to care for us. I wept through my first few nights there. One of the mothers had already had her baby, a daughter and was caring for her for six weeks prior to adoption. We all adored that child. After seeing the terrible sadness experienced by that mother when the time came to part with her child, I made the decision that, when my turn came, I would allow a foster mother to care for my child for the six week period prior to adoption. Later that evening the young mother returned still holding her baby. She had been told that the day had been changed and could she return the following week! I advised the Adoption Society of my decision and they tried to talk me out of it, by telling me that it could be harmful for a new-born baby to be separated from its mother. Yet, simultaneously one was being told that keeping one's child was a very selfish act!

However, I stuck to my decision. The Home was a refuge owing to the closeness of the mothers. We shared our secrets and our hopes with each other. We were even sometimes able to laugh together. We all had chores to do. We did the housework and worked in the kitchen and we all had to attend mass every morning.

As it came closer to the time for my baby to be born, I was told that they were going to try to turn my baby from the breech position. This took place under a general anaesthetic, but when I came to, they told me the attempt had been unsuccessful. I went back to the Home and was vomiting blood. The next morning I was rushed to hospital in an ambulance. However, I recovered and was returned to the Home.

Finally my turn came and I realised my contractions had started. I was alone in labour and a bit frightened. When they brought my daughter to me, I was immensely proud. I had to stay in hospital for two weeks and was able to care for her in that time. I was delighted that I spent her first Christmas with her. My sister came to visit me and shared my joy and pride. We lived for the moment and didn't think ahead to what was to become of my child. I sent a telegram to my parents which read, "Pink parcel safely delivered." After a few days, reality hit me and I began to be sad about the thought of parting from my beautiful daughter. I was allowed to breast-feed her. The nurses were sweet and kind and the other mothers were gentle with me also.

Finally I left the hospital and my sister found me a bed-sitter to live in. I visited my daughter regularly in her foster home. I felt very alien, being back in the 'normal' world. I found it hard to face people who didn't know my secret and pretend. I tried to socialise, but I found myself shy and strange and especially reluctant to talk to men. Within ten days of leaving the home I had another job in a department store.

I used to visit my daughter every Sunday and paid the foster mother for the week to come. I lived for those Sunday visits and often arrived at the house in tears. Every Monday I rang the Adoption Society to find out what was happening, only to be told that it was 'difficult' to find adopters for her because I was 'a foreigner'. Every week I watched my child grow and develop, smile and laugh at me. She was such a joy to me and I began to indulge in thoughts which had been in the back of my mind for so long – that I might, after all, keep her. After all, my family was 'well-heeled', I had a job, I had friends.

Finally, when my daughter was four and a half months old, the Adoption Society told me that they were in contact with a society on the island that I come from, with a view to having my child adopted there. I was enraged, because I knew that if she was adopted on my island, I would surely come to know where she was. This would be unbearable for me. Finally I went to a different agency. They found a home for her very quickly.

Then I started to have serious doubts and to wonder if I could, after all, keep her. Then I remembered the lectures I had had at college, telling me that adoption was the only way to provide a secure future for my daughter and the best possible chance in life. They had told me that my child would benefit from having a mother and a father like all the other children. The Adoption Society told me that it was cruel and selfish for me to waver in my resolve.

I finally said goodbye to my daughter when she was almost six months old. Three months later I returned to London to sign the papers in front of a Justice of the Peace. They explained to me that even then I could change my mind, but I knew that it 'wasn't right' to do that. I knew that my father and my aunts would help me out if I decided to raise my daughter and I loved them for that. However, the deed was done and after the adoption was finalised, my daughter belonged as much to me as she did to any stranger in the street. I would like her one day to know all of this.

I became obsessed with the fear of getting pregnant again. I also had a huge fear of walking in the dark. I used to walk in the middle of the street, as I was terrified that someone would jump out and grab me. These fears, the fear of being raped and the fear of becoming pregnant, haunted me for several years. They will never leave me completely.

~~~

Jenny's son was born in England in 1962

My story leading to the loss of my dear, first son began in mid-1961, in England, where I was born and grew up. I became pregnant shortly after my seventeenth birthday, while still at school. I was in a steady relationship and felt loved and cherished by my boyfriend. But, as my parents' only child, there were high expectations of me and our relationship did not have their approval. My boyfriend and I naïvely assumed that we would marry and so when I eventually confessed to being four months' pregnant and told my parents of our plans, an enormous shaming and blaming process commenced. I didn't know then where adopted children came from, but I was soon going to find out!

All the decisions were made by my parents, who threatened court action should I go against their wishes. Despite the initial support of my boyfriend and his family, I was swept along the path arranged by my parents and the family solicitor and was dealt with by children's services social workers, as I was considered a child myself, twenty-one being then the legal age of majority in England. The formal adoption occurred under English law some months after the birth, but I was not permitted to know the date that this would take place, just instructed closer to the time to sign the papers. Still legally a minor, but perversely old enough to sign away all rights to my baby! What a contradiction, but, of course, always marginalised!

I felt helpless and my boyfriend, no doubt, also felt powerless, but he being a few years older it seemed to me then that he took no initiative. Soon also he virtually abandoned me. In the process of the bitter exchanges which followed the news of my pregnancy, my boyfriend and his family withdrew their support. Further shame and blame were heaped on me and apparently I was deemed to be solely responsible for being pregnant!

I was quickly banished far away, first to stay with relatives whom I barely knew and for the last weeks of my pregnancy, to an unmarried mothers' home in another distant town, again hidden from anyone who might know me. My misery and loneliness throughout were immeasurable. The other girls and women there were also consumed by what they were to face; we did not have the emotional energy or the knowledge to help each other. My losses included what had been a loving relationship with my boyfriend, my parents' respect, my friends, my schooling (or the beginning of adult life at work) and the general fun of spreading my wings, not to mention loss of self-respect and my sense of self. Nobody ever asked how I might be feeling. I did not know what to expect through pregnancy and labour and I felt totally isolated and deserted.

My baby was born in 1962; nobody but me to treasure him, nobody to share the experience with me and nobody to help me give him the welcome into the world that every new baby should be entitled to! No presents for him or flowers for his Mum. The procedure in the home where I stayed was that mothers looked after their babies for about six weeks until an adoptive family was chosen – by the adoption agency of course! There was never any suggestion that there could be an alternative to adoption. All the powers colluded in the process of removing a baby from his unwed mother and transferring him to a 'deserving, married couple'. I do recall that my baby's father and I met in a nearby park so that he could see his child and there was a sense for me of this being somehow important. I also thought I might be helped to escape from what was going to be a traumatic parting from my baby. I can remember nothing of what was said between the two of us, but it was a measure of how he felt that he travelled several hours by train to see us. Of course, no one knew of the meeting and I cannot recall how we arranged it. I was completely numbed by my experiences.

The time spent caring for my baby was a joy, though the cloud of our pending separation was huge. A letter arrived with a few days' notice instructing me to take him to the adoption agency, which was two hours' drive away. My parents fetched us and my memories of sitting in the agency's waiting room where my baby was taken from me can still, after forty-eight years, flash clearly before me. I still experience the feeling of that moment of loss in my body. My baby slept throughout, even as he was carried away, out of my sight, but, of course, never out of my mind. My mother was with me, my father waited outside in the car and no emotion was shown by either of them. I was expected to go home and get on with my life.

Comfort in my grief was denied and my sorrow was seen as lack of gratitude for being allowed to return home, rather than being banished forever from the family. I was forbidden to discuss it with others. I had brought enough shame to the family. Sometimes in the years to come, it felt as if my baby had not been real.

I learnt very well to conceal my pain and to remain silent about my experience, so that the episode remained an almost buried secret for many years. It almost became unspeakable and many other emotions were locked away in the process of containing within me a huge aching emptiness. I was haunted by who and what my baby faced when he awoke, haunted by his going to strangers not of my choosing. I was the only mother he had known and not only had I bonded with him during my pregnancy, but for two months I tended his daily needs as we two lived in a kind of limbo, a sweet but poignant interlude immersed in a precious shared time. He responded to me, his mother, with his first smiles. What a sweet, soft and responsive little fellow he was, what a priceless gift for that 'deserving, married couple'.

Nothing prepared me for what would follow, the yearning, the searching, the gaping void. A coping mechanism for me was to imagine that his adoptive parents and I shared a common warm thread of connection. This was to be later well and truly destroyed, when they were hugely affronted that I should try to contact their son (my son) in the 1990s, when he was well into adulthood. The English system, through an intermediary agency, marginalised me yet again, when insisting, against my wishes, that they would contact his adoptive parents first, so that they would not feel left out. This process confirmed an English system that still considers natural mothers to be of least importance in the triad, an unequal system born of moral judgment.

Yet, how lucky I felt later when I eventually allowed myself to feel again and reflected that there was one small part of my son's life that could not be taken from me. I did indeed have some tangible and very much cherished memories of my son's first two months of life. Whatever should happen, in denying me the opportunity to bring up my first son, no one could ever take away those precious memories of his first weeks and first smiles. Those memories are so precious and they belong only to me.

Women in my position were not to know that the shame imposed on us, through the transgression of societal mores of unmarried motherhood in the 1960s, would alter in another era, to become the shame of having given away our own babies. How could a woman worthy of the title of 'mother', ever do such a thing? But we mothers who lost our babies all know how we were repeatedly told at the time, "If you love your baby, you will do the best you can for him and allow him to go to a couple who can provide for him." We were supposedly unable to provide what our babies needed, because we were single and unsupported.

Then and now

My grandchildren, accustomed to welcoming all babies who arrive into the family, no matter the marital status of their parents, were initially confused by finding they had an uncle as yet unknown to them.

After years of thwarted efforts at the hands of the various reticent and secretive agencies to whom my records and those of my son had passed and then more frustrated years after my son had rejected all ideas of knowing his natural mother, I was thrilled that, at forty-five, he finally decided to contact me, wanting to know me and hopefully start to build a relationship. The smile of my dearly loved baby was immediately recognisable and the essence of him is very evident in the man he has become. Words cannot describe how fortunate I feel that we have reconnected and are strengthening our relationship each time we meet.

Will it ever be quite enough? Can I ever recover what I lost? I will never have the role that was denied me all those years ago, but I do now have my son in my life. He is real. He is getting to know the families he lost and his natural mother's family is enjoying what we have so far and can anticipate in the years ahead. So, although our relationship can never be what it should have been, it doesn't prevent us making the most of what we have, which is a warm and meaningful reconnection.

Many uncomfortable feelings have been ameliorated by the personal work I have done over the years by digging my secret out of its toxic place. This has brought me to a greater openness surrounding my adoption issues, enabling me to resolve much of my shame. Then a few years ago, before my son reconnected with me, I arranged a meeting with his natural father to share information that I had gleaned about our son over the years. This also brought some relief of feelings and a degree of peace. Very importantly, he expressed his sorrow for the part he played in what I had lost as a mother – a further healing for me.

I now have reached a stage where there will always be some aspects of my grief that may prove difficult to resolve.

I can accept its presence as a normal reaction to what was an abnormal and cruel situation for any young mother to endure. I can also accept myself in the process and begin to understand that what took place was a reflection of the era. This all helps to dull the pain etched in my body and my psyche.

~~~~

Mara's son was born in England in 1966

The world was my oyster in 1963. I was about to leave school and walk into full-time employment, courtesy of my beloved cousin, Jeanette, who was manageress of a business. Believe me, full-time employment was extremely rare in Stranraer, the small, seaside town in the south west of Scotland, which was my home.

I was introduced to the company accountant, Hasan, who explained the mundane business of tax and national insurance contributions, which I protested at a little. Being so green in the work place, I complained about working the long hours proposed for £2 10 shillings in wages. However, the money belonged to me; I worked for it.

I was also very green when it came to forming relationships with the opposite sex. I didn't realise I was being wooed by Hasan. The last thing on my mind was love. I was so full of being independent, wanting to save for all sorts of adventures. Buying my own clothes was a real priority, as wearing hand-me-downs was a country-wide practice. After about six months, I finally went out on my first date with him. I challenge anybody to tell me, that falling in love for the first time in life is not the most wonderful experience. Yes, the world was beautiful with my rose-tinted glasses.

It is now 1966. I am pregnant, on a train, leaving Scotland for this country they call England, which I only know through geography lessons at school – banished, broken, terrified – and all because I fell in love, in the wrong era, with the wrong man, who was the wrong colour and religion.

I never saw my son's father as 'coloured'; I just saw him as this lovely person I had fallen in love with. I now have to don the mantle of the fugitive, for my sins.

The mother and baby home is far enough away; the only means of contact is by letter. I conjure up in my mind – caring Christians – as it is a Salvation Army Home I am heading for in Newcastle-upon-Tyne; it was called *Hopedene*. Austere is an understatement; we were all in a high anxiety state continually. We were never greeted with kindness. I was described as 'the Scots girl with the half-caste baby', even when we attended the local hospital for injections, where we were kept apart from the 'normal' patients.

This comes back to me in my flashbacks, in my dreams; a never-ending abyss of fear and sorrow. While I was in the home, Hasan was sent to his homeland to take part in an arranged marriage. He promised to set up a trust fund for me – I suppose that was to be some kind of compensation – but it didn't happen.

The bedrooms, up in the attic, were freezing cold and we got one bath per week. There was no pre-natal care or instruction and the food was atrocious. We were made to work hard. All we heard was, "Are your chores complete? Where are you working next, girl?"

We were marched to the Salvation Army temple every Sunday like children and we were made to sit on the 'penitence' benches, where the whole congregation could see us. We were the goldfish in the bowl of gossip.

With the full onslaught of labour, I received not a single painkiller. I was told that I had to suffer for my sin. I was screamed at for coming off the bed when told not to, then caught again and slapped hard for not doing as I was told. In the advanced stages of labour, I was made to wipe up the mess I had created when the enema decided to evacuate at the bedside.

The two officers at my delivery were, I believe, qualified midwives, yet I never received ante-natal care or proper aftercare. Because of their negligence, I have attended gynaecologists and urologists from 1967 to this very day, with a number of unsuccessful operations, different treatments and medications, but to no avail.

My beautiful baby son was born at 9.00 pm, but the evil two took him from me immediately and told me I would not see him until the next day. I was not even allowed to touch or hold him. It was the longest, darkest night of pining and pain. Yet, in my soul, I wanted to tell the world that I had this beautiful baby. I remember hoping that his father would hear my soul crying for him to come and rescue us from this nightmare. I was trapped in this hell-hole of a place, with no means of escape.

I was forced to try to breast-feed my baby, even though I was in pain. When that didn't work, I was given high doses of Stilbestrol, to dry up my milk. I became very ill, but no one looked after me. The babies, from the age of one week, were fed a teaspoonful of custard or semolina, with the 6.00 pm feed, to fatten them up for adoption.

Life continued in this vein; incarceration under a penal servitude regime. My son was three months old, when I was told that they had adopters for him and he would be going soon. That struck such fear in me – I just could not believe it. Then some days later I was told they would not be taking my son, as they wanted a perfect baby and they had noticed that he had an eye defect.

My baby was getting older. Policy only allowed us to be with our babies at feeding time. The rest of the time they were under the care of staff. Yet often I heard him crying. He was separated from the new-borns and in a room entirely on his own, with absolutely no stimulation, dark, drab and grey with torn bed sheets and blankets. Because he had no toys, I started to knit some and I knitted three pram sets for him with matinee coats, bootees, mittens and hats. I did extra chores for the girls and they paid me sixpence and so I bought wool.

During my year of incarceration, I received only one letter from my father. I never received a single letter from my mother.

Breaking the rules brought heavy punishment. I broke them often, by sneaking into my baby's room to cuddle him and play with him. When I heard the footsteps coming, I hid under his cot. I was just eighteen years old, still quite innocent in life. When I was caught, I was banished to a place called North Ashfield (a so-called 'women's hostel' – actually a 'doss house'), until the adoption took place.

"Well, well, girl, you will be glad to know we are having a Christmas fair and there will be potential adopters coming to buy at the fair and so for the few days and nights it takes place, you will take your working clothes off, dress yourself nicely and the baby nicely and look smart."

I was dressed smartly and my son was dressed like a Christmas turkey for the buyers. Bingo! My son's adopters saw us, made inquiries and so the ball started rolling. They had a teenaged daughter; she came and saw him and I was told that she wanted him for Christmas. Meantime she was told she could choose a name for 'their new baby'. She chose the name Kristopher, because he was her Christmas 'gift'. Since that time I have hated Christmas with a passion. When I read the Bible, true Christianity shines forth, but I never experienced it the whole time I was in the supposedly Christian home. Since learning that Pope Gregory chose the 25th of December to be Christ's birthday because it was the date of a popular pagan festival, I realise the parallels between Christmas and adoption. Both are based on lies and a false history.

"Now, no tears. You are the luckiest girl. Your baby is going to a family that has businesses. He will never want. He will have a real mum and dad to care for him and he has a teenaged sister to spoil him. You are so lucky, girl. Now go and do your chores with a glad heart." I can't get over the cruelty of this evil exchange they call adoption. I was ushered into a room and told to dress my son in new clothes.

I wanted to dress him in the lovely clothes I had made for him, but I was told not to be silly, because that was not what the adoptive parents wanted.

The zombie mode has kicked in; I am dying on my feet. I am shaking uncontrollably. My beautiful baby is anxious. "What's up, Mummy?" is what his wee face is saying to me. "Please, Mummy, don't cry". *Oh God, please God, help me, I can't go through with this. My baby is nine months old; he is my life. Please come and get me, Hasan. Our baby needs us.* My strength is gone. An angel appears, in the form of a Scottish Salvation Army officer and she is with me. She is a real Christian. She weeps with me; she sees my baby so upset at me crying. She holds me and we weep together. I feel a real physical pain thrust through my heart and that's all I can remember.

I could not sleep. They watched me for the next week, then told me I could go home after another week. I had to wait to make sure the adopters were happy with my baby. They had to keep me busy and I had to keep doing my chores so that I would 'forget' about my baby. I had to wash down walls and paintwork throughout the officers' quarters. My nightmares were of my baby standing up in the cot, his arms outstretched for me to pick him up and when I reached for him, he disappeared. They are as vivid today as they were forty-four years ago.

I returned home, to be told by my mother, "Don't unpack your suitcase. You will be off in a day or so. You can never live at home ever again." I was given £50.00 and told to make my own way in life and to take my secret to the grave.

I was beyond pain by then, beyond feeling; death would have been such a comfort. My father walked with me to the bus station. I headed for the first bus to Glasgow and was there within five hours. I stayed at a women's hostel.

Then and now

This was my punishment, for falling in love. No one ever told me what my rights or entitlements were.

Never in the history of the human race, has an act as cruel as adoption been devised. To me, it is the worst transaction in the history of the human race and it should be banished to the annals of history.

Suicidal, I was sacked from my first two jobs in Glasgow, for crying at work. I locked myself away in my room in the hostel. I attended the doctor for stomach pains; he told me that I was wound up like a corkscrew and gave me antidepressants. I suffered all my life with ulcers and now have a cluster of polyps, also severe irritable bowel syndrome and nervous anxiety. I became anorexic and Mogadon and Valium became my friends, to help me make it through to another day. Since then I have lived daily with a 'living bereavement'. It truly is a bottomless abyss of sorrow.

Reunion with my beloved son was the final dregs of this poisoned chalice. It was like a precious healing stream, full of euphoric love and joy, to touch my baby again after almost forty years. I longed for my son and I to get to know each other, to have the odd day here and there together, but that was never to be. Unfortunately, he has no intention of getting to know me; he never wants to discuss adoption – past, present or future. He keeps his distance and prefers to talk to my husband and his siblings than get engrossed in conversation with me.

I feel as if I am a part of his life that he would rather be without.

All I ask is to have my beloved family in my life and for me to be a mum and a granny to them, but reunion has taken my beloved son and my only daughter, as she has been deeply affected and has not had contact with me for four years now. I have two grandchildren I have no contact with – all because I fell in love and made love.

Adoption has taken all my life and my mental and physical health. It has torn my family apart. I cry out to God each day, "Please, bring my son, daughter and grandchildren home to me."

~~~

Ros's son was born in England in 1968

My story is, sadly, not unusual for a teenaged girl in England's sixties. Seventeen and pregnant as I prepared to sit 'A' level exams at school, my parents were shocked, angry and ashamed. It's interesting that although it was 1968 and the age of 'adulthood' was then legally twenty-one, the few documents I was made to sign then were those which denied me the motherhood of my son, at ten days old.

There were no choices; it was made clear to me by my parents, doctor and the social services who organised the adoption that I was unfit to be a mother, would receive no support if I tried to keep my baby and – what sounded like a genuine argument then – that if I truly loved my baby I would demonstrate that love by giving that child away, to 'a responsible, deserving married couple'.

I had known my baby's father D for over a year and we were engaged. He was just finishing school and had a university place for later that year. Our parents separated us; D was sent off on a long holiday and I was virtually imprisoned in my bedroom, warned that neighbours and visitors must not see me. I had just one prenatal visit to hospital, as my mother was determined I would become invisible.

Baby S was born in N General Hospital. I was frightened and totally unprepared for the birth and was admonished by one nurse for 'making that dreadful noise'. When S was born and put next to me I was amazed at the simultaneous waves of love and anguish that drowned me. I whispered, 'hello' and his solemn, dark brown eyes seemed to observe me as if he knew that we would soon be parted. The rules were that I stay in the ward for ten days alongside the 'real' mothers who deserved their babies and would be keeping them. I fought not to receive the shots that would have dried my milk and secretly breast-fed S, against the rules for mothers such as me.

After three days I was so miserable that I walked out of the hospital with my son tucked inside my school blazer and went to D's parents' house, knowing there was no welcome for me at home. D's mother reluctantly accepted me into her house where I stayed until the Social Services came and took my baby away on the tenth day.

There was the sense of a huge sigh of relief at home. It was as if my mother felt a mess had been cleared up and we could all get back to normal; my parents never again referred to my pregnancy or their grandson. Meanwhile, I slipped into despair and depression. I went to university on a teacher training course and there hit rock-bottom, attempting suicide. I am eternally grateful for my friends there (the few who knew my terrible 'crime') who saved my life. I turned to alcohol, promiscuity and risk-taking. I would have welcomed a sudden end to my pain.

Three years after S was born I married his birth father, for the wrong reasons; D knew my dreadful secret. How could I get close to someone else and have to tell them what I'd done? Consequently the marriage was uncomfortable and built on loose foundations. By choice there were no more children. For me, it would have felt like a betrayal of my first-born.

I would never have disturbed my son's life by searching for him, even though not a day passed without my thinking of him. All the missed birthdays, the landmarks in his life – I had no idea even if he was alive. This was a tightly closed adoption.

111

ADOPTION SEPARATION

Then, in 2006, NORCAP (a UK charity reconnecting those parted by adoption) contacted me on behalf of my son, now an Australian, who was searching for me. My life turned upside down and still feels that way at times, almost four years on.

It is only in these past three years that I have come to understand the damage I did to my son and I deeply regret it. A baby needs its natural mother – they are still a unit, after all, even though the birth has taken place. Parting mother and baby is like amputation of vital parts, for both of them. Each may learn to live with their disability, but can never fully recover.

I am glad that we now live in times where unmarried women are no longer considered wicked (though this still pertains in some countries) and where they get help to stay with their child. But the legacy of our 'crime' lives on; I live in England and on applying for an Australian parent visa was told, 'You have no connection to this person. You do not qualify as his mother.' So in the eyes of the law I am still not my son's mother.

The ripples of adoption spread far, wide and ceaselessly and the harm done by this most unnatural of man-made acts is vast but still, largely, concealed. Many thousands have been affected, directly and indirectly in several countries. The more their stories are told, the greater the hope that such inhumanity will be abolished.

How it happened...

...in Ireland

ADOPTION SEPARATION

Cathy's son was born in Ireland in 1971

"You are very welcome. From now on, your name will be Cathy, for as long as you will be with us." That was my introduction to The Home for Unmarried Mothers in the early seventies in Ireland.

The nuns gave us complete anonymity. No one would know who we were. I had said goodbye to my family, who were ashamed of me. Now I said goodbye to my identity. Would I ever get used to hearing myself called Cathy? I wondered, did I look like a Cathy?

I was shown my bed, one of three in the room. Funny, but I can't remember anything of the first few days. I believe I was in shock at finding myself in this 'home', where I would stay for the next five months until my baby was born and adopted. Naturally, there was no question of *not* giving my baby for adoption – wasn't that the reason I was here?

Gradually, I made friends. We were such a mixed lot – from every background under the sun! We bonded together, much like prisoners, I imagined, especially when labour pains came.

Immediately, we clustered together and prayed for whoever's turn it was that she would be OK and safely deliver her 'little one'. I felt terror in my heart every time some one went 'down'! How would it be when it was my time? There were two lay midwives assigned to attend our births. One was known as 'the frightful one' and the other as 'the angel'. I worried about which one would deliver my child.

We each had a job, which whiled away the long hours. Some cleaned the rooms, others worked in the nursery, others got a job in the local community.

The nuns were very kind and arranged whatever suited us. I opted for a job outside. I was placed in a home attached to a little country school. It was a disaster. I was expected to wash the floors in the little country school every day – there were only two rooms in it – but when the work was finished, I was expected to stay in my room – out of sight and out of mind. The teacher and his wife never spoke to me. I didn't exist for them. It was a chilling experience.

I 'phoned the convent after a week or so. Could I please come 'home'? Imagine begging to get back into that Home! Fortunately, the company of the other girls banished the loneliness of that cold house.

I got a job in the nursery. It was lovely helping to feed and wash the babies. The only problem was that the mothers minded their babies until adoption – which could take up to four weeks, sometimes more. This allowed plenty of time to bond and then it was heart-breaking to let go.

One girl I made friends with shared my love for literature. We used to go for long walks in the lovely grounds around the convent and passed the time by quoting out loud every poem we knew, from Wordsworth to Milton and every speech from Shakespeare we could remember. I thanked God for the nuns who educated us and insisted on us learning off by heart!

The dreaded labour pains came eventually. I had mixed feelings. I told myself it meant the beginning of the end of my captivity. The peculiar thing was that I was free to leave that home anytime. But go where? Back to England where I had become pregnant? That was definitely a 'no-no'. I knew the baby wasn't safe there. It was too easy to have an abortion.

When I discovered I was pregnant, the local doctor offered me an abortion. When I told him I couldn't have one, (even though I wasn't a practising Catholic at the time, it was out of the question for me) he thought I couldn't afford one. He offered to give me the money and told me I could pay him back by joining a group of other Irish girls he had signed up, who 'obliged' his friends. He was a pimp! I walked out and knew I wouldn't survive long in London. For the baby's sake, I decided I had to go home, no matter what the consequences.

I suppose I expected my mother – when she got over the first shock, to come around, but she never did. It was banishment to The Home for Unmarried Mothers, in the country, so that the neighbours wouldn't know.

At that time in Ireland, unlike now, there was no recognition for unmarried mothers and no allowance from the government. If the family didn't support a mother and child, it was well nigh impossible to keep the child, unless the mother had a good enough job to employ a nanny. Crèches were unheard of. I was jobless, moneyless and had no confidence in myself that I was fit enough to rear a child on my own. There seemed no way out, but to give my baby for adoption.

So here I was in labour, praying for a safe delivery. How easy it is to pray when in dire straits! 'Dear God, help me through this – give me a healthy baby.' Night came. I have no idea how long my labour was – it seemed so long. Of course, the midwife was 'the frightful one' – 'This is all your own fault; so stop complaining'! They were the loneliest hours of my life, but joy comes with the dawn. My baby was the loveliest boy ever!

He was beautiful, with blond hair and blue eyes. I wrote home with the good news, asking my Mam and Dad to come and visit me and see my baby before he went for adoption – some hope. Definitely not! How strange – it is only as I write this that it occurred to me, that none of my family visited me the whole time I was in the home.

Six weeks later I handed my baby over for adoption. I have no recollection of physically handing him over. All I can remember is standing in a corridor with him in my arms, praying to the Blessed Mother to take care of him and to place him in a good home, then everything goes blank.

I have no recollection of going home to the city. It was weeks later that I 'came to' and then the tears started. I got a job and tried to start a new life. There was never a mention of my baby at home. It was all swept under the carpet, as if it never happened.

Seven years later, out of the blue, my mother said: *I think we made a mistake about the adoption.* I was so shocked that I was speechless. That was all that was said – end of story. My mother died suddenly a month later.

I wrote to The Home for Unmarried Mothers every time I moved address, for when, if ever, my son wanted to contact me. Some hope, I thought; but he did, many years later. But that's another story!

~~~~

Olive's son was born in Ireland in 1971

My story of pregnancy and loss began when I returned from Paris in late 1968, after spending a year there. It was the most wonderful year of my life. When I returned to Dublin, I got involved with a man who had also been abroad and so we found each other at a party at a friend's house and, being young and having the same situation of being abroad for a year in common, we found each other interesting. We spent lots of time together and had great fun. We were both the same age, twenty-three years old.

As we were still very young and I was still exploring my life, the next year I went to London and Spain for a couple of months and we were still very much in touch with each other while I was there. When I came back from Spain we picked up where we left off and continued going out together. It was at this point that I got pregnant. We had been using protection and so it was a shock.

From this point on, my life changed forever. I went to the doctor alone to have the pregnancy confirmed and it took ten days to get the result; it was positive. I was shocked and elated at the same time. I was shocked, because, in Ireland at this time, it was very much frowned upon to get pregnant outside of marriage. I was also elated to find that there was a life growing and that I was going to be a mother for the first time and, as it turned out, the only time.

The father was not interested in keeping our baby and suggested an abortion. At that time and even now, there is no legal abortion in Ireland and I would have had to go to England to get one there. I had never considered abortion.

This was my first child and I wanted to find a way of keeping it. Firstly, I was sacked from my job, because I was pregnant. Then the father got a transfer to work abroad and so I was pregnant, scared, with no job, no money and the father of my child was gone. I felt abandoned. There was nowhere to turn to for help in 1970.

I ended up living with a family in the country for the rest of my pregnancy. This was a family suggested to me by a priest and they had two adopted children. Most of my own family were living abroad at this time, except for my mother, who was seriously ill. I never told her I was pregnant.

When my son was born, in 1971, they wanted to take him away from me straight away, even though I was in a private nursing home. They never brought him to my room and so I had to sneak down to the nursery to see him. I had no way of bringing him home with me, because I didn't have a home to bring him to, as I was living with this family in the country. The priest came to see me and recommended I have my son adopted, as it was the only way he could have a good life. I was nowhere in the equation at all, not even considered good enough to raise my own son. I left the nursing home and my baby was taken away.

119

For the next three months, I tried every way I knew how of keeping my son. I left the country and got a job in Dublin and I tried to find an apartment where I could have my baby with me. This proved to be very difficult, as they didn't rent to unmarried mothers at that time and if they did it was usually a damp basement. Also there was nowhere for me to place my baby while I was working. At this time I was working and visiting my son in the home and trying to find a way to keep him. There was a lot of pressure from the social workers for me to give him up for adoption. I was made to feel that the longer I left it, the more damaged he would be. In the end I found I had to have my son adopted.

I had lost what I thought was a loving man, I lost my baby to adoption, I lost myself and I lost the potential to realise my dreams. I had lost the rite of passage to be a mother. There was no celebration for me, just shame. Then the process of stuffing my feelings down began. There was no such thing as therapy. They didn't recognise how damaged I would be after such a trauma. I had no one to talk to about my experience, because everyone was busy telling me to get on with my life. They spoke as if the loss of my child was so easy to get over, just like a toothache.

I moved to Canada in 1978. I worked in the Travel Industry as a Tour Manager and had the opportunity of travelling to many places around the world, which was wonderful. It was while I was in Canada that I started therapy and after many years of therapy and working with a support group for birth mothers, I felt I could start to look for my son and the possibility of a reunion.

I met my son, in Dublin, in 1994. I had been living in Canada since 1979. The date I met my son was the 26th of June, to be exact. It was the most wonderful day of my life, after years of not knowing anything about him – twenty-two years, to be precise. For weeks before the meeting, I was fully alive for the first time in years.

Friends and colleagues were telling me that I looked different; much more at peace with myself and younger-looking too!

My son and I had corresponded for a couple of months, before speaking on the 'phone to each other. All of this contact was wonderful for me. The next year we met at a friend's apartment in Dublin and had privacy for an hour or two. My son brought along photos and I showed him some of my photos too. As the hours ticked by and turned into many hours, my son asked me if I would like to have dinner with him. I was thrilled. He booked a little Italian restaurant in the neighbourhood. We spent the entire evening there and, in fact, they were sweeping the floors around us as it was closing time and we hadn't even noticed.

The next day my son wanted to meet me again for lunch, which we did and it was very enjoyable. During this time of our reunion my son's adoptive mother was calling him on his mobile 'phone, but I hadn't noticed much, as I was so caught up with our reunion. Not long into our reunion my son mentioned to me about organising a meeting with his adoptive mother. I wasn't ready to meet her just yet and I tried to stall for time, as all I wanted at this moment was to gain some level of time with him and develop my own relationship with him. It had only been a few days and it was a precious time for me, but his adoptive mother was persistent and my son was going in to bat for her and so, in the end, I gave in. I went to meet her and his adoptive father, a week before I left to go back to Canada.

I found the whole meeting too much. It was just overwhelming! His adoptive mother didn't seem to understand the effect meeting them had on me. She showed me photos of their life together, not just recent ones, but baby photos as well and the tears were streaming out of my eyes. I had no control over them. She said, "I thought you would be happy that your son had such a good life." I found it painful to have to try to explain my tears and sadness. I was in terrible emotional pain and it was all so raw and so I decided that it was time for me to leave. My son was understanding, but seemed much more concerned with his adoptive mother's feelings. I didn't feel like anyone had really seen me or understood what I was going through.

Our reunion was a three week moment. We parted on good terms, or at least I felt that we had. As I have always travelled back and forth to Dublin almost every year since I started living in Canada, I came back the next year on my usual visit with the additional desire of visiting my son again and getting to know him a little better. In the meantime my son had got involved with my cousin's adopted daughter and, by the time I arrived back, the following year, they were already in a relationship. He had written to me telling me about getting involved with her during the year.

When I arrived in Dublin, nothing I did was right; at least that's how it felt to me. My son really didn't want to see me at all and was very angry with me and didn't want to spend time with me. In fact they went away for two weeks together while I was in Dublin. It all became very stressful and messy. When I asked him what was wrong, he became verbally abusive to me and the two times that I did see him, he was very verbally abusive and attacking. I found the whole thing very difficult and painful. I did try to speak to him, as to why he was so angry with me. He just seemed to get angrier and he continued to become even more verbally abusive. So in the end the best thing to do at this point was to leave it.

I didn't come back to Dublin the following year. I spent time with some dear Canadian friends instead to help balance and heal myself in beautiful Victoria, British Columbia. I was very emotionally and physically drained after that last meeting with my son and it took me a while to bounce back to any kind of normality. I never saw him again.

I moved back to Dublin in 2001 and, after a couple of years, I tried to contact him again by letter, to see if we could start afresh. He wrote back to tell me that he didn't want anything to do with me and to stop sending him messages or cards, that he was just curious and his curiosity had been satisfied. My cousin's adopted daughter and my son broke up after about four years. To lose my son once as a baby was very hard, but to lose him again as an adult was even more difficult and the very worst part of all was to be denied knowing my grandchildren (two of them, a boy and girl). They are now, I think, five and eight. I only heard about him getting married and having children through the grapevine.

I struggled with the pain and loss for many years. I can't begin to tell you what it was like to have my son say he didn't want anything to do with me.

I've come out this side of this terrible trauma with my sanity almost intact, with good friends and family support. Even though my connection with my son did not continue, I am still very glad I met him.

Maybe one day he will want to know me. Until then, all I can do is hope. In the meantime, I am going on with my own life and it's good and sometimes even very good.

I wanted to write the story of my reunion to see it written down for myself and for women like myself, who do not have contact with their children who were lost to adoption and lost again after reunion.

~~~~

Louise's daughter was born in Ireland in 1989

It was Ireland, 1988. I was sixteen. Single mothers were looked down and frowned upon, a mixture of pity and 'what a waste' mentality. The Catholic Church still held a tight grip on the minds of the people and its influence should not be underestimated in regard to how single mothers were perceived.

I can still see the look of disgust that clouded my mother's face when she discovered I was pregnant. I was warned not to dare mention it to my friends. How could I have when I believed I had committed the worst sin imaginable and I was the scum of the earth? My sister never brought the subject up. My younger brothers were never told until years later. The issue was what other people would think and say. This took precedence over what was best for my baby and me.

I remember my Dad coming into my room one evening, crying and telling me how he had spent the evening driving around wanting to drive off the end of the pier. He cried and hugged me. This was the only emotion I saw from my parents during my pregnancy.

I was brought to the doctor only once in my first seven months – not in broad daylight, of course, but to his house in the next town. My Mum was assured that it would not appear on my medical records; oh, if it could only be blotted out so easily from my mind.

CURA, the crisis pregnancy agency, was contacted and a meeting arranged, of which I have no recollection. Abortion, of course, was never an option and never brought up. At seven months I was sent away to a Mother and Baby Home run by nuns, for the duration of my pregnancy.

As awful as this sounds, it was heaven when compared to the atmosphere I had to endure at home. I could finally breathe again. I was with girls in the same situation as I was and felt accepted for the first time. The homes were run by the church, which 'fed' these babies into the Catholic-run adoption system and into the homes of more 'deserving', childless couples.

It was reiterated to me time and again by the adults I trusted, parents, social workers etc, that a baby was better off being brought up in a two-parent household. This made no sense to my young mind, when I lived with my Mum and Dad and sure wouldn't there be two adults in my house? However, I couldn't have even considered any options and so I couldn't let myself 'go there'. I had to block it out – not think of the awful predicament I found myself in. This was the only way I could cope and get through it.

I knew I couldn't keep her for so many different reasons. I was never asked what I wanted. My mother arranged it all. I was just scared and wanted everything to go back to the way it was before. The shame this would bring on my family was more than my parents could bear. I remember the extent they had gone to, to hide my pregnancy.

Mum was told that admission to these homes depended on places available and so I was expected to be grateful for any help. I remember her telling me that I could sleep on the floor, if needed. I was portrayed as the one that had created this situation, while the mother and baby homes, the adoption agency and the adoptive parents were my saviours, to whom I should be eternally grateful.

When I lost my daughter to adoption, I often remember thinking that people get more sympathy and support when they give away pups. I had no after-care, nor was I ever offered any. I was sent back to school and told that I could put it all behind me. I believed them. How wrong they were.

I was only a child myself and this trauma affected every aspect and subsequent decision in my life. In my opinion, this neglect was nothing short of child abuse.

I buried my feelings as best as I could, told no one and stayed 'emotionally frozen' as such, until my daughter turned sixteen. That's when my feelings refused to stay down any longer and reared their heads demanding that I acknowledge them. But that's another story.

ADOPTION SEPARATION

Then and now

How it happened...

...in New Zealand

ADOPTION SEPARATION

Gary's son was born in New Zealand in 1967

I was born in New Zealand. I spent my childhood and the adolescent years north of Wellington, on the North Island. My eldest son was born on the South Island in 1967. He was raised by adoptive parents, who were local people. In 1969, I left New Zealand to pursue a career. Now, I am a resident of Australia. The son I lost to adoption continues to live not far from where he was born.

The New Zealand in which I developed was a conservative nation. The two+two nuclear family was the norm, mirrored by the unit that was my father, mother, sister and me. For many of my parents' contemporaries, Britain was still viewed as 'home', even though these people were, in many instances, second and third generation New Zealanders. Britain offered another security; it was the market to which New Zealand sent its butter, meat and wool. Our prosperity was tethered to the appetites and the climate of the mother country on the other side of the world. We as a nation believed that we were 'God's own' (sometimes 'Godzone'), which was reinforced by the title of our national anthem, 'God Defend New Zealand.'

Life was comfortable, even predictable. We were a staid family unit within this stable society. I cannot recall getting into trouble, apart from breaking a neighbour's window and inadvertently killing a tree at school, but these were hardly serious misdemeanours. I remember, as a teenager, being told by my father that there was no more noble personal pursuit than 'being a good citizen.' I was disappointed to hear that this was Dad's aspirational summit. I thought that for an adult (and especially my father) the goal was mundane.

ADOPTION SEPARATION

Looking back, I realise that for the first twenty years of my life, unknowingly I had adhered to this maxim. In general, I had been compliant. In the academic sphere, where I excelled, I was known as a quiet achiever. The innate traditionalism of the New Zealand community and a 'don't rock the boat' attitude within my family influenced the events that unfolded in 1966 and 1967.

I met Kay in 1966. We were both university students. We fell deeply in love and planned to marry. As the result of our passion, we created a child. From the moment that Kay told me the news, the damning phrases 'illegitimate' and 'conceived out of wedlock' began to resonate, unbidden, in my head. Kay was adamant she could not tell her strict parents that she was pregnant; their high hopes for her would be dashed. The spectre of thwarted expectations was raised also by my father: how would my doting godparents react, what about my beckoning career as a geologist? Denied the key support on two parental fronts and feeling that I failed in the male mission to find a solution for our incipient family, I panicked. Fright became flight.

Kay finished the university year and moved across Cook Strait, well away from her unsuspecting parents. However, we continued to write to each other throughout the pregnancy. We met in Wellington soon after our son was born and the adoption formalities had been completed. She told me that being spared the wrath and disappointment of her parents in no way compensated for the profound sorrow she felt when her son was taken from her immediately after she had given birth, without her ever being able to hold him. Years later, I read that as a punishment for the single mother's sins, typically the baby was whisked away to the sanctuary of the hospital nursery, which the 'fallen' mother was forbidden to visit. In Kay's case, a sympathetic nurse, disobeying orders, allowed her to view her infant through the nursery window.

I asked Kay what she had called our son. She had bestowed one of my given names, because, she said, "I love you." I was flabbergasted. I had let Kay down, yet she bore me no grudge. I felt that I did not deserve to be exonerated and on this note, in May 1967, we parted. A year later, I found out that Kay had married; I suspected that constancy was one of her husband's virtues.

Of course I have reflected on what happened in 1966/67. Yes, I had been incapable of rising above the prevailing community stigmas and ingrained family attitudes. But there were fundamental flaws in the decisions I made, particularly from an ethical perspective. I had acted selfishly, intent on self-preservation. Most of all, the woman I loved deserved to be treated as the most precious person in my life. In this essential demonstration of devotion and trust, I failed.

During these ambivalent times, I remember contrasting reactions to two relevant events. Only once in my life have I felt the urge to punch another person. This occurred in late 1966, when my best friend, who happened to attend the same university as Kay, made derogatory comments about an aspect of her behaviour, based, by his own admission, not on observation, but hearsay. Then in 1968, in my final year at university, one of the Honours geology students had a child by his long-time girlfriend and ... they stayed single and raised their baby boy. Mick was the first person I had encountered who had chosen to stay a single parent. Nobody in the class ridiculed or avoided him. Secretly, I admired his moral fortitude.

For twenty-one years, I denied that I was a birth father. Then, in 1988, two adoption-related events occurred. On the day that I thought might be my New Zealand son's birthday I experienced the irrational reaction, that he, having come of age, could not lay claim to me as his father. A long suppressed unfounded notion that, at any time during my son's childhood, I could have been served with a maintenance order surfaced after twenty-one years. Now that he was independent, I no longer was 'responsible' for him. My rational self reasoned that I was relieved of this burden. Before we met, my wife, Helen, had given birth to a baby girl, who was raised by adoptive parents. When an adult, she searched for her birth mother and found Helen. Perhaps, in turn my son would search for me. I knew that I was not ready to face him. First, I needed to resolve the disquiet I felt.

For a while, I did nothing. Slowly, it dawned on me that my dissatisfaction with my career, my parenting skills and myself was quite possibly linked to my failure to deal with the momentous events of 1966/67. The more consideration I gave to this connection, the more likely, then certain, it became. I knew nothing of my son's adoptive names and therefore his whereabouts, but it seemed I could search for and find Kay. At another level, this sequence made sense. I had let Kay down and I owed her the apology I had not made a quarter of a century earlier. Through checking the electoral rolls, I located Kay. I visited her in New Zealand to say sorry face to face. Kay was moved by my initiative. As I had not been present at the birth and thus was not on our son's original birth certificate, only Kay could make enquiries about him. A few days later, she received and passed on non-identifying information about Mark, raised by parents who had been in their forties when they adopted him. These people were the same vintage as my mother and father!

This time, Kay and I stayed in touch. The first action I undertook was to add my name retrospectively to our son's original birth certificate. I did not want him to find a nil entry under 'Father' or worse still, 'not known'. I required Kay's signature as her endorsement of this rectification. She told me that this was a significant undertaking on my part, adding, "We are in this together, now." Having added my name, legally I was in a position to contact Mark.

Kay and I made a point of speaking by telephone on Mark's birthday each year. During an additional September five hour marathon conversation, we revisited the events of 1966/67 and made our peace. We agreed that our rapprochement had prepared us well for our respective possible reunions with Mark. In 2009, finally I met Mark for the first time. I had sent him birthday cards for the previous decade and he responded positively to my June invitation to get together when I visited New Zealand in November of that year. He suggested that we meet for the first time in a coffee shop, which happened to be the setting I had long imagined for an event that became a landmark in our lives. Kay has chosen to wait until Mark is ready to make an outreach to her. I have told him that Kay would welcome his contact, but the decision about when he takes this action is his alone to make.

Mark has told me that he does not blame Kay or me for his adoption. When in the mid-1990s I told Helen's and my children about their half-brother, they welcomed the disclosure. Friends and extended family took the revelation of my birth fatherhood in their stride. Maybe, my assessment of my actions has been conditioned by the social mores of the time when the conception and the adoption took place, whereas recent recipients of the news are making their judgment against today's more liberal outlook. If so, these differing interpretations reinforce the need to educate the community about the era when bastard children and single parents were ostracised.

During the search for my self and the two other members of my birth family, I have made personal discoveries. The original separation by adoption resulted in a loss; by undertaking the searches, I endeavoured to understand the repercussions of the resultant grief and to incorporate these into my life. I have learned that reunion is incomplete without the involvement of the birth father. To me this is no surprise, because all three members of the birth family played some role in the events surrounding the adoption, were wounded by the same episode and so stand to benefit from taking individual and collaborative measures to heal the pain.

133

Furthermore, I found out that when you initiate contact, you do not know the degree to which the other person has undertaken personal healing and so it is best to proceed cautiously. Overall, in the aftermath of adoption separation, perseverance, allied with generosity and patience can pay dividends.

Two of the most critical decisions of my life are related to the one event. Losing a family to adoption is the nadir; eschewing denial, acknowledging my adoption experience and reaching out has broadened my horizons and, as a bonus, drawn me to my present vocation, the first job I have been passionate about.

Today, I accept I cannot undo a deed that resulted from my human imperfections and had far-reaching consequences. However, the way I think and feel about my adoption experience has changed, for the better.

Informed by what I have learned as a birth father, I have written three books about adoption.

[Gary is currently employed as manager of a post-adoption support service in Australia.]

~~~~

Sylvia's daughter was born in New Zealand in 1968

This is a story I thought would never be told. I don't ever think about it, because it horrifies me and I've certainly never talked about it.

I was living at home with my parents when I discovered that I was pregnant. In the social climate of the 1960s, telling them was not even an option. Desperate times call for desperate measures and an illegal abortion was preferable to having a baby out of wedlock. I knew someone who had friends in low places and through his underground contacts he was able to get me some pills, that were supposed to cause a miscarriage. Oddly, they were black. I was alone when I took them all.

134

Then and now

I wondered what was going to happen, but I would deal with it because I needed not to be pregnant.

The pills did not work and so my low places friend took me to a so-called doctor in a rundown area of a neighbouring city. It was night time when we pulled up in front of an old, three storey home. I had been told to enter through a side door and was led to a room with an examining table. This table had a roll of paper at the top that could be pulled down to make it fresh and sanitary for the next patient, but I was greeted by paper with doodling on it. I paid the man and bent over to receive an injection of something. Again I wondered what would happen, but nothing did.

Now my desperation knew no bounds, as I was in the fourth month of my pregnancy. My low places friend put me in touch with a taxi driver. I was instructed to go to an area of town I was not familiar with at all. I was to meet him alone in a stereotypical 1950s-style cafe. Part of me must have been terrified, but mostly I was numb. I was there for five or ten minutes when a short, fat, round-faced, unshaven, balding man approached me. I was easy for him to spot, because I looked so out of place. We left the cafe, got into his cab and drove for a while. Then I was blind-folded, because I was not to know where I was being taken.

When we arrived at the destination, I was led to a room and told to lie down on the bed, naked from the waist down. Still blind-folded, I could hear footsteps and voices and I could feel hands on me. Then a faceless man douched me with an unknown solution. I don't remember the trip back home where, again, I waited for something to happen. Would I expel a lot of blood and chunks, or would I go into labour and give birth to a foetus? Whatever was going to happen was going to take place in the little bathroom in my parents' home. Again, nothing happened.

I was definitely not in my right mind – I was in sheer panic mode. Nevertheless, around my parents I was an expert at hiding my feelings and acting like all was well.

Unbelievably, in my desperation, I would make one more attempt. Now I had my own friends in low places and I contacted the taxi driver myself. This time they would make a house call. For some reason which I cannot recall, my parents would not be home for a while. This time I would be lying naked from the waist down on my own bed, with a pillow over my face. Again I was only aware of footsteps and voices and being touched, when a solution was being pumped into me.

This attempt failed as well and I came to the conclusion that this baby wanted to and would be born.

Looking back, I am horrified at my naïvety and at the risks that I took out of fear and desperation. I could very easily have been hurt and, of course, the same applies to the child I was carrying. The knowledge of this haunted me throughout my pregnancy. Happily, my child was born whole and healthy. She was adopted soon after her birth and I have never told her this story.

~~~~

Wendy's son was born in New Zealand in 1968

I am a multiple relinquishing mother having given birth to and relinquished four babies (including twins) before having a tubal ligation at the age of twenty-eight. My thinking, (if you could call it that) was that I wasn't prepared to have any more babies that I couldn't keep. It took a further fifteen years until I was made aware of the fact that I had, in my desperate confusion, mutilated myself. I was a statistic: no more, no less.

Then and now

I am a single woman, who lives alone. My closest relationships are with my two (desexed) cats. I am anti-social. I trust very few people and so, by default, am untrustworthy myself.

I have met my eldest son, who is now forty-two years old. We love each other dearly, but our mutual fear of rejection made it necessary for us to take things very slowly and carefully. I kept having to remind myself that this young man was not my lost baby. That baby is gone forever.

Having suffered various abuses as a child, I had begun stealing at a young age as a way of trying to 'feel'. I was numb, you see and the adrenaline rush when I stole something, helped me to know that I was alive. When I was eight years old I was made a Ward of the State and so began an upbringing of institutionalisation. Foster homes did not take, as I had such a huge mistrust of people, particularly families.

So at sixteen and a half I found myself pregnant, alone and hundreds of miles from my family, to whom I was a virtual stranger. My baby's father had been arrested as an illegal immigrant and never knew of my pregnancy or the subsequent birth of our son.

Anyway, I immediately ran true to form and began shoplifting once again. I was caught, of course and sentenced to a Borstal Training period, 'not exceeding two years' at what is now Arohata Women's Prison at Tawa, just out of Wellington, New Zealand. I was four months' pregnant at the time. Many years later I retrieved my files under the Freedom of Information Act and discovered that my pregnancy had been the leading factor in my incarceration! Oh well.

It seems like I spent a large part of the next five months scrubbing. All of the prison floors were raw, sanded timber. We girls kept it clean and shined to a deep, rich gloss by scrubbing. We each were issued two scrubbing brushes. One was for use with hot soapy water and the other was for dry scrubbing ie scrubbing along the hand polished raw wood grain until it gleamed.

First, the knees blistered, then broke; bled, scabbed, bled some more and finally blistered again. Thirty years on I still carry the scars on my knees; one of many.

I was locked alone in my cell the night I went into labour. It must have been midnight when the first pain occurred. It was a timorous thing at first, weak and uncertain, although it didn't stay that way. At some point I knocked on the wall and woke up Annie, the girl in the next cell, mostly to have someone to share this with. She panicked and began to pound on her door and scream for the night staff. I giggled as I calmed her down. Here I was in labour, she was terrified on my behalf and there was a wall between us anyway. It all seemed very bizarre and quite unreal.

When the night staff did their next check they allowed me to have my light on so that I could get my things together and so I carefully refolded the already perfectly folded layette that I had prepared for my baby. It was pretty meagre. I earned twenty-five cents per day operating a commercial mangle in the prison laundry, which didn't really allow for any extravagant spending. My baby's layette consisted of three lovingly smocked and embroidered nighties in soft cream winceyette, two knitted singlets, two pairs of pilchers, a matching jacket and leggings, six pairs of bootees, two helmets plus one and a half dozen nappies. It was not a lot.

The night passed until at last it was 6.00 am and my contractions were close enough to warrant a trip to the local maternity hospital, Kennepuru. After being 'prepped' – what a euphemism for a shave and an enema – I was put into a room alone to wait for my contractions to acquire the intensity necessary to the birth.

Now, because I was afraid, I was also frozen with it and my body would not work. It seemed to want to keep the baby within itself and although I was having contractions every two to three minutes, they simply weren't strong enough to accelerate the birth process.

The hours passed and, although a nurse would pop in from time to time, nobody actually stayed a minute, or spoke a friendly word. I was in labour a further twenty-three hours and grew more and more distraught with fear and stress; more so than the actual pain, I think. It was a nightmare.

Finally as the sister was yelling at me to, "Shut up, you great big baby – you're disturbing the other mothers", my waters broke and from there things began to happen very quickly. I remember through a bright yellow haze of theatre lights the doctor and nursing staff dressed in green, rolling me onto the theatre table, pushing my knees up and my legs apart, ordering me to 'push, push' and so I tried and just as my son's body slipped from mine, I caught a glimpse of the nurse beside me, poised with a hypodermic.

I screamed and sprang up in the bed and lashed out at the nurse, knocking the needle to the floor. Another nurse grabbed the baby and I had a flash of dark hair and tiny limbs then the nurse's bulk hid him from me. "It's a boy", I heard. "Give me my baby!" I screamed and burst into tears as someone took my precious bundle away through another door.

"That child is up for adoption!" the sister snapped. "He bloody well is not!" I collapsed back onto the bed and after the placenta had come away and the doctor had stitched me up, ("Two internal and two external", he remarked brightly), I was once more taken into a room by myself.

I honestly cannot be coherent about the days that followed. It is a nightmare blur of different faces, threatening, placatory, false-friendly, stern, all arguing that my son would be better placed for adoption. The Child Welfare, (I was still a State Ward), the prison counsellor, the hospital matron.....

I retreated into a stony place and then planted myself firmly. "I'm not signing any papers and you can't make me." There was nothing else I would say after a while.

ADOPTION SEPARATION

My father came as soon as he could. At the time he was working on a hydro-electric scheme in a remote part of the country and came out of the bush by helicopter, taxied a hundred miles to the nearest airport, then flew the eight hundred miles or so to Wellington before taxiing directly to the hospital.

They refused to let Dad see his grandson, just as they kept refusing to let me see my son. Dad's outraged roars could be heard reverberating throughout the building, but the Matron was firm. I was a State Ward, therefore my son was also the property of the State and the Child Welfare had instructed that my son be kept apart from his mother and also his grandfather; in fact, any blood relation. 'So sorry. Not my responsibility'.

Dad and I held each other and wept together.

He could not stay. He had got time off on compassionate grounds and was expected back at Deep Cove. I was on my own again.

I took to hanging around in the corridor outside the nursery, gazing at the bundle in the crib marked 'Baby James'. I was coldly polite but very firm in my maintained refusal to sign adoption papers. I was in hospital for ten days and, during that time, I was never once permitted to hold my baby. A nurse took pity and went so far as to hold him up to the glass for me to see – strictly against instructions – and, oh, he was so beautiful with his softly curling hair and dark, liquid eyes. Oh my little sweetheart. I am going back to prison. What will become of you?

I finally got to hold my son when he was three months old, for half an hour in a cold prison visiting room. He looked more afraid than anything else, or maybe it was my fear projecting outwards. The prison social worker as well as a visiting Welfare Officer were still trying to convince me to sign adoption papers and I had no knowledge of my son's whereabouts, knowing only that he was somewhere in foster care.

Two months later I was released after having served ten months of my 0 - 2 year sentence. Jimmy, my baby boy was delivered to Arohata in time for me to take him with me to catch the plane for Invercargil about eight hundred miles south.

My father had quit his job at Deep Cove and I was to move in with him. It was very difficult. Jimmy and I were virtual prisoners in the house. I kept house for Dad and tended the baby. Dad provided a roof and food for us. I had no money and no means of earning any, occupied as I was with Jimmy, who was a delight in every way, just as I had known he would be. At first, things seemed to be OK. I had my boy to compensate for lack of friends or money (there was, of course, no single supporting parent's benefit) and Dad seemed to be OK. Then the arrangement began to fall apart.

My father has always had a volatile temper and the stress of being totally responsible for Jimmy and me financially was beginning to tell on him. He began to hit the whisky bottle and his language and behaviour at home became increasingly more violent. Finally I spoke to him about it, saying that although I loved and appreciated him for his efforts, I could not have Jimmy at risk of being affected by Dad's increasing lack of self control.

It was at this point that my father attempted to kill me. Whether or not it was deliberate, the result was the same. While Jimmy slept in his cot, my father tried to strangle me. Fear lent me the strength to fight him off and I managed to flee to a neighbour's house from where I called the police, who came and spoke to my father, who told them that he'd caught me in bed with not one, but three men, hence had beaten me for this.

Well it was a total lie, but worse, I was the one with the police record and so obviously I was not to be believed. The police officer who spoke with me simply said, "I'd give you a hiding if you were my daughter too, you little slut. Serves you right" and left.

The bruises about my throat and face didn't come out until the following day and I was too afraid to have any further contact with the police. They didn't believe me anyway.

ADOPTION SEPARATION

I watched the house carefully and when Dad was due to leave for work, I returned to see to Jimmy. I was at my wits' end. Too afraid to stay with my father and having no means of support, I turned to the Child Welfare for help. The only help they were prepared to offer consisted of them taking my baby away into foster care.

I guess I went a little crazy about then. With Jimmy in foster care, my father immediately packed his personal belongings, locked up the unit preparatory to selling it fully furnished and caught a plane for the North Island leaving me homeless, childless and on the edge of a breakdown.

Within a week I had been arrested for 'Disorderly Behaviour' and sentenced to a further term of 0 - 2 years. Now, my parents had divorced when I was three and my mother had returned to Britain. Although she came back to New Zealand when I was nine, I hadn't had much to do with her and had certainly never lived with her.

When I was sentenced once more, I came to the point where I felt Jimmy should not be parcelled around from home to home any more. My feelings didn't matter, as long as he could have a safe and happy home and one permanent mother and so, when he was twenty-two months old, I gave up my fight to keep him and signed the necessary papers.

Many years later when we found each other again, I learned that Jimmy had been hugely abused by his adoptive parents, his adoptive mother being the active perpetrator and his adoptive father helping to protect his wife from the world, by ignoring her brutality towards my son. So much for self-sacrifice and hopes for a better life for Jimmy.

At forty-two years of age he still suffers the emotional effect of my relinquishment of him as well as his subsequent abuse. He has little to do with his adoptive family (the mother is dead) and has chosen to live in the South Island of New Zealand close to my family, although he rarely sees them.

Then and now

He called me Mum at first and we were in constant touch with each other, but a huge barrier seems to have grown. I had hopes that some day I might get to be a grandmother and have the opportunity to spoil the children of my son, but now it seems unlikely. It feels as if, no matter the effort, I shall never be able to compensate for his loss or mine. We are both fully aware of this and so our relationship has been bitter-sweet, marred and scarred by trauma that no amount of goodwill can 'kiss and make better'.

At the moment I have had to distance myself from him emotionally, for my own well-being. There is no end to this story. Perhaps its purpose is to educate and maybe help some other mother to a further understanding of the ways in which the system helps to steal our children if we are not on constant guard. At any rate, I hope this is of some use to someone out there.

ADOPTION SEPARATION

How it happened...

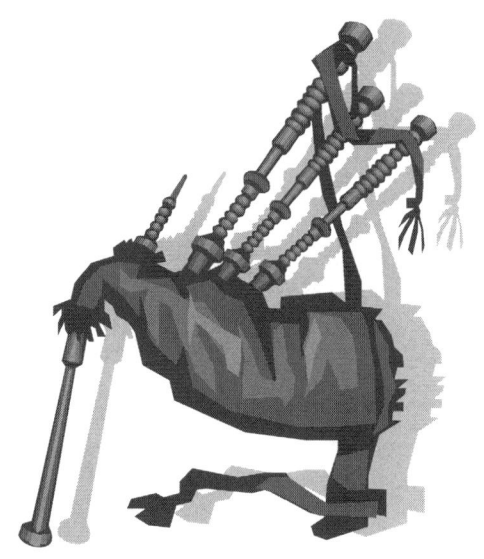

...in Scotland

ADOPTION SEPARATION

Then and now

Sadie's daughter was born in Scotland in 1962

I had just left school in Paisley, Scotland at fifteen years of age and was in secretarial college.

I had started to go out with a boy who seemed much older and street-wise. After a couple of dates I lost my virginity to him and became pregnant. It seems very naïve now, but I really was very uneducated about sex (my mother told me that I knew what was right and what was wrong). Finding out I was pregnant was terrifying and my mother realised what was wrong and after searching around Glasgow, a home for unmarried mothers was found for me (Glasgow's Home for Deserted Mothers!). The home was in West Princes Street in Glasgow and had a large brass plaque outside saying 'Home'. I am not sure who ran the home but there were some bibles around. I have since tried to find records of the home, but none seem to exist.

It was arranged that I would go into this home when I was about two months' pregnant, give birth and then the baby would be adopted at six weeks old. I never questioned my parents' decision to make these arrangements and it seemed the only solution. The option of keeping my baby was never suggested, although my mother later said she often regretted the decision. I know that my parents acted in my interests, although, of course, nowadays this would never happen.

I remember feeling devastated when my mother took me into the home and when she left we were both in tears. She visited me regularly and I was taken on outings, but really I was hidden away from friends and family, so that I could return home without anyone knowing where I had been for six months. Only a very close aunt and uncle were told.

My mother made sure I kept up my secretarial studies whilst in the home and I took in a little portable typewriter.

The Home itself was like a Victorian workhouse. We were wakened early and given breakfast then had to do household chores all day, including scrubbing floors and carrying heavy coal buckets upstairs to the 'Board Room'. We also had to go outside to the laundry room and light the coal-fired boiler and then do all the washing in the freezing cold laundry. This work went on until confinement and there were many cases of housemaid's knee. We were only allowed one bath a week, but we used to take a second or third turn in the bath water of others.

The home had a staff of three. The Matron ran the home assisted by a nurse who was really quite unpleasant, saying things like, "The change of life didnae change me." She also once accused me of stealing thread from the sewing room, when she found me hemming a coat with sewing materials my mother had brought in. She was in charge of our health, supposedly and then was in charge of the babies when they were brought back from the hospital and placed in the nursery, which was on the top floor of the home.

There was another little Asian lady who was the 'cook'. The food was pretty disgusting and most of mine went down the toilet. The roast beef on Sunday consisted of a slice of mainly fat with very narrow circles of beef. There was also a smoking room in the basement, where many of the girls smoked. The other girls were actually good fun and we all came from completely different backgrounds. The overall feeling was that we had done something terribly wrong and the staff treated you as such.

When you went into labour you were taken to Robroyston Hospital to give birth and stayed there for a week. It was a complete eye-opener for me and I was beside one woman who was giving birth to her eleventh child. There were many screams and cries and prayers from women in labour and this terrified me.

Then and now

The birth itself, though obviously painful, went smoothly and I then set about trying to look after my baby.

We were not allowed to breastfeed and were given tablets which would dry up our milk. I was stunned and amazed at the maternal feelings I had, as soon as I held my baby (a girl) and I had to choose a name for her (Shirley). I remember a very well-off lady next to me who had lots of visitors and flowers, but she seemed pretty hopeless at looking after her baby and asked me how to change a nappy. My only visitor at the hospital was my mother.

After a week I was taken back to the home and there I looked after my baby on a strict regime of feeding every four hours. I used to love the middle of the night feed, when I seemed to be completely alone with my baby and although I knew I had to give her up, I had never felt such feelings of total love.

After six weeks, I looked out of our dormitory window and I am sure I saw the prospective adoptive parents of my baby leave one day with a little boy. A few days later my baby was taken away from me and I never saw her again. I have no idea who adopted her, although I vaguely remember being told that they lived over in the west of Scotland (possibly Argyll). The night before I left my baby in the nursery for the last time, she smiled and gurgled and I spoke to her incessantly.

I was then taken back home to live with my parents and no one ever spoke of the event again. Once, when I appeared upset, my mother said I could talk about it any time, but I was never able to. I had such feelings of loss and hopelessness. I have thought about my baby every day since. She will now be forty-eight and although I have tried to trace her, I have had no success. My only hope is that she will someday contact me and I have left my details on the contact register at Birthlink in Edinburgh.

ADOPTION SEPARATION

Edith's daughter was born in Scotland in 1968

My story began in 1946 on VE (Victory in Europe) day really, when a young Scottish Nurse and an American Pilot in the Canadian Air Force got together.

They were engaged and the celebrations took an intimate turn. Some time after that the pilot was sent home to America and the young nurse found out that she was pregnant. Her parents were horrified and, more to the point, didn't want their daughter marrying a foreigner – especially a brash American.

No letters arrived. Our nurse waited and waited for the post every day; nothing. Her parents decided it was better that she hide away in the house, only going out in the dark for a short stroll and being upstairs when there were callers.

Still no letter arrived.

March arrived and baby Anne was born. All was well and our nurse took her baby home, but not for long. In a few weeks some people came to the house and Anne left her side forever, or so she thought.

Baby Anne was taken to see her new parents, oblivious of the heartache left behind; they were older and had tried for a child themselves. They became pregnant nine times, got to full term and were delivered of grossly deformed babies that didn't live long. Today they would have had genetic counselling, but not then. The advice would have been to go away and try again. Anne's name was changed to Edith by now.

Edith grew up, did well at school but could never understand that feeling that something was missing. She didn't know what it was, just that feeling of a space where a part should be. When she left school Edith became a nurse, not knowing that she was following in her mother's footsteps. She often asked about her background, but never got a reply of any consequence. It seemed that no information was available or was being held

150

back. All her questions did was cause anger and she would be sent to her room to think about what she was asking and the hurt she caused. One day she overheard her Mother say to a friend, "Of course, Edith is adopted. We don't know how she will turn out; she could have bad blood."

Soon Edith herself got engaged to what her parents thought was a highly unsuitable guy and she found she was pregnant.

I am Edith and this is my story.

I so wanted that baby, someone of my own to love and to cherish and to love me, but all Mum and Dad could think about was the shame and the gossip. I was taken to see the local minister of the Church of Scotland and spoken harshly to about the shame I had brought on my family and my village. It was agreed that I would be taken to Glasgow to a Mother and Baby Home called Landsdowne House. It was run by the Church of Scotland. I arrived and was shown into the sitting room, where there were rows of chairs with girls of all ages in various stages of pregnancy, sitting knitting and looking sad. That was to be me, I thought and waited outside matron's office to be admitted.

The interview was harsh – very harsh. How had it happened, where had it happened, was it only once or had it happened many times, who had it happened with and how many of them were there. There was disbelief when I said it had happened with only one person.

The routine was harsh too; housework, scrubbing stairs, even when in labour, but the worst of all was when the Women's Guild would visit from one or other church. They looked at us like animals in a cage – the fallen ones, all lined up for them to see; a lesson in sinning. No absolution here then, no kind words, just looks of utter disgust.

I remember even with all that, wishing my pregnancy would never end. You see, you were mine and I knew that whenever labour started the process of me losing you would begin. I wished that day away, but it came. I went into labour and was sent to scrub the floors, until I could no longer bear the pain. Then I was sent to hospital. I remember no one talking to me, except to ask how the pains were. I remember being looked at with disgust and horror, as if I had two heads or maybe I was the scarlet woman.

Anne was born. It was a warm, July day in 1968. Yes, I called my little girl, Anne. I had no idea that was my birth name.

I remember my father visiting. His message was clear; either come home without Anne and care for my Mother, as I had been trained to do and pay my debt to society, or never see my family again and have no help or support from anyone. I felt that I wanted the best for Anne and obviously I was not fit to be a mother in other people's eyes and I believed it. I was crushed. I had breast-fed and nursed Anne for a few weeks, then nothing; she was gone and I had an empty hole for a heart.

When I got home there was no mention of my experience; "no tears here", I was told. My Mother had breast cancer and it had spread to her lungs and she was dying. I nursed her and cared for her until, in November, she died. Grief kicked in – for my Mother, who had cared for me and for my daughter, that she didn't want to know and I would never get to know.

I never had a post-natal check-up; I was an unmarried mother and so it didn't matter. I landed in hospital, very ill. A piece of placenta had been left behind and became infected. The Doctor said I must be pregnant again; after all that's what 'people like you' do. I didn't and I wasn't, but, because they delayed, I nearly died. At the age of twenty-six all this resulted in me having a full hysterectomy. It was 1969.

I decided to go to Aberdeen and do my maternity training. Nothing like meeting grief head on, I thought. It was hard, but I pushed my way through it and no one knew what went on behind my eyes or at night when I was alone – the intense grief. Through all of the years that followed I thought of Anne every day. I spoke to her as if she was here. I told her I loved her and missed her and I hoped in my heart that she was well and loved and cared for.

Many years later I found my own natural Mother. She was in Australia and still is, aged ninety-one and I have two sisters. We have met and get on well, considering the distance between us. They came to visit for my sixtieth birthday; it was wonderful. Four generations of one family together for the first time. Yes, four generations – Anne had found me. It was in 1991, my father was in hospital and I was living back at home temporarily taking my stepmother to hospital to visit. It was early May and Dad was dying. On the way home from hospital one day, I had a really strange feeling; I knew there was a letter from Anne. I just knew. I told my Stepmum and she said, no, I was torturing myself because I was about to lose my father. I was right. Behind the door was an envelope addressed to me as my maiden name and in it a photo of a girl, who looked just like I had at that age and a baby boy, her son.

I sent a telegram back saying, *I love you* and giving her the 'phone number. She 'phoned that night. We talked every day and eventually she felt secure enough to visit. It was wonderful, but hellish when she went away; it was like losing her all over again. Now I sit in the middle of two families, unable to be a complete part of either, but happy for the bits of contact I have.

For those of you who want to adopt, remember we birth mothers want the same as you, to see our children happy and loved. We are no threat to you; don't see us as the enemy. We are part of your children's past and they need to know what makes them how they are. If they ask you, let them look, let them find and let them make up their own mind as to how it goes from there. They will love you all the more for letting them be themselves.

ADOPTION SEPARATION

Shelagh's son was born in Scotland in 1970

My adoption story does not have a happy ending, but my intention in writing it is to tell my truth, hopefully to inspire and encourage other mothers like myself who relinquished their baby for adoption and to continue my own healing from the deep trauma that was for many years unacknowledged and hidden.

My story starts in a similar way to many others – I became pregnant in the summer of 1969, between leaving school and starting university. Even in the so-called swinging sixties, social attitudes to sex were still judgmental and society unsupportive. Pregnant at seventeen, unmarried, ineligible for any welfare benefits, it was hard to take in the overwhelming consensus that abortion, or adoption, were the best choices available to me.

My parents were shocked, angry and distressed, but eventually supportive. In the end I made the decision to relinquish my baby for adoption, believing that it was the best thing for him to be with a family in a secure, loving home, which I could not give him at that time as a student in my first year at university. It was the hardest thing I have ever done, except of course for giving birth alone and half unconscious, calling out for my Mum.

It was hard at the time to understand the harsh judgment of social workers, doctors and nurses, for whom I developed a long-lasting distrust. Looking back now I think they did their best – it was part of the social culture of the time. I think we all did our best to make sense of what seemed intuitively wrong at a basic human level.

I moved on and tried to put my guilt and pain behind me, as I was encouraged to do. There was no mention of counselling and probably little understanding at that time of post natal depression. I carried on with my life, graduated from university, married and was fortunate to have two more beautiful children and my life seemed on the outside to be fine.

However I had kept a secret that was gnawing away inside me. I never stopped loving the child I had relinquished and often thought about him and the deep love and loss I had experienced. I suffered from depression, I drank too much, worked too hard and eventually I began to break down, unable to keep down the desperate feelings I had been working so hard to avoid.

Even then I didn't realise that I hadn't grieved.

Eventually I plucked up the courage to tell my own children the story, (my husband had always known) and also to start the process of trying to find my first son. The outcome of that search was that he couldn't be found – meantime I found some healing and much needed forgiveness, for myself and others. I let go and held an open space in my heart for him to find me when he was ready. I acknowledged his birthday every year by giving a present to someone through a charity.

Just after his fortieth birthday, I received a letter from an adoption social worker who wanted to visit me. I was alarmed and excited and for twenty-four hours my mind made up every possible scenario about what this could mean. I knew from my experience of supporting a friend whose relinquished daughter suddenly turned up in her life, that it's not always easy. I also thought of much worse scenarios.

After forty years, I learned that my son had died when he was only fifteen. I was told only that he had died in an accident and given an apology that the adoption agency had not discovered this fact when they did their initial search for him.

I felt a whole mixture of emotions in quick succession: sadness, anger, despair, numbness and my mind reeled with questions and accusations. But I was left only with new information and little support available from the adoption services. The social worker later apologised to me for giving me this piece of news and then effectively leaving me to deal with it on my own.

Sadly there still seems to be a gap in adoption services for the support of relinquishing mothers from many years ago, a seemingly forgotten third of the adoption triangle.

I felt primarily a sense of loss for his death, for the loss I felt when we separated and for the loss of my hoped-for reunion with my adult son. All the old emotions, memories and hurt opened up again, stronger than ever and this time I really grieved, with professional support and a growing understanding of the unresolved, buried grief I had carried for such a long time.

I also did my own research and discovered my son's adopted identity and the real, tragic circumstances of his death and what seemed like a breakdown in his social care. It could have been easy for me to blame myself – as if I could have prevented it by not giving him up. I thought I had made a deal – if I make this incomprehensible sacrifice, that will ensure that my son will be OK. Sadly, that was only fantasy. I have learned that I can deal with my emotions and the consequences of my actions. I make more constructive choices when I face reality, as it really is, not what I wished it could have been.

I now see that there was never a guaranteed happy outcome. I do know that he was loved by a family for most of his life. I may never know the full story of my son's life; I have no rights to that information. I can't bring myself to approach his adoptive parents, as I know they must have suffered too and I don't want to open up old wounds for them or cause them any more distress.

Although my grieving is not complete, I feel free to move on with my life, even now in my own sixtieth year. I am not bitter; there have been times when I was, but not any more; resentment only contributed to my own misery and had no effect whatsoever on the people I resented. I am lucky; I married and have two healthy adult children and found a high level of happiness and fulfilment in my life.

Then and now

I don't need to carry a burden of guilt any more. Actually I never did need to feel guilty. I did the best I could at the time.

In my recent healing I have found gratitude for my life and for the gift of life I gave my son. I am grateful for the precious, short time we had together and for the family who loved and cared for him the best they could. I believe that he was in my life for a reason and that I learned of his death at this time for a reason. It is time for me to fully forgive myself and be free to live and enjoy my life, without guilt and resentment holding me back.

The simple truth is that I was his mother and he was my son; I loved him and still do. I gave him his life and did the best I could at the time, trusting that it would be enough. I am grateful that he was adopted by a family who loved him and I share in their loss. I hope that we may all find healing and forgiveness in our own precious lives. All is well.

~~~

Mary's son was born in Scotland in 1977

I gave my son up for adoption in 1977. I am married and have been blessed with another three children whom I love more than anything in the world.

I had polio when I was little and wear a leg brace. But when I got to my teenage years I had a very low opinion of myself. I never had a boyfriend and when I was about twenty, I met a boy who had a drink problem and a police record, but he was interested in me and I thought: *If this is the only boy interested in me, then I'd better go out with him.* He treated me very badly. He hit me and was generally unkind, but I was grateful that someone wanted to be with me.

Anyway, I ended up pregnant and that is when I woke up. I did not tell this boy that I was having a baby because I had to protect my child.

My parents threw me out of the house and for a while I stayed with a brother and his wife who were not really child-friendly. I planned to keep the baby, thinking selfishly that I had someone to love who would love me back.

At about six months pregnant I realised that I had nothing to offer a baby – no home, no money and no back-up support.

A baby did not deserve this. I decided to have him adopted. I have never felt such desperation or loss as on the day I gave my little, beautiful son away. I don't regret it from his point of view, but from mine, I regret it every day and wish there had been another way.

God was good to me and I finally met a lovely man, got married and had three wonderful children – all grown up now. But never a day goes by that I don't think about my first son.

There isn't much after-care for girls who give up their children and I always felt that once my son was adopted the adoption society had what they wanted and I was of no interest and no one enquired about how I was coping.

I was told many years later that I should have received a photograph of my son, which I did not get and when I tried to find out how he was doing, the adoption society told me that the family had moved and they could not contact them.

Sometime later a nun started to work at the society and she got in touch with the adoptive family and got a photograph of my son and told me they were living in the same place and that they had never moved. I never understood what that was all about, but I was so grateful to that nun.

How it happened...

...in the United States

ADOPTION SEPARATION

Linda Lou's son was born in the US in 1965

I was fourteen when I got pregnant in 1964. I was already repeating 8th grade because my grades were so bad from the year before. I am not dumb or stupid; I was repeating 8th grade because I was stubborn and would not study. My parents were embarrassed by this. We lived in a small town in Ohio and failing a grade was just not acceptable.

It was early October when my Mom noticed that I was not having my periods. She asked if I could be pregnant. Of course, I told her, *No*. One day after school, I walked outside and my Mom was waiting for me. I figured something bad was going to happen, because Mom did not drive and she had to walk to get to the school. I wanted the earth to open up and swallow me. I just knew Mom was going to walk me to our family doctor. I was mad and embarrassed. I was not happy to see her. We walked in silence the two blocks to the doctor. Back then you did not have to make appointments; you went and signed in and waited for your turn. Mom explained to the doctor, the same one that delivered me, what was going on. He looked at me like I was trash. He did the pelvic exam and leaned over me about two inches from my face and said, "You are that way." I will never forget his eyes.

He turned to Mom and told her not to worry, because he knew what to do with me. I thought that he was going to make me not pregnant any more, but instead he was telling Mom about the Florence Crittenton Home (FCH) in Toledo. He and his wife had adopted a girl from there about fifteen years before and he knew that he could pull some strings and get me in right away – and that is when the story began.

He said that it was a blessing that I had failed the year before, because they could take me out of school right away and

161

say that I was being sent to Notre Dame School for girls in Indiana, to make sure that I studied and passed that year and to get me ready for high school. I was pulled out of school and had to sit at home until FCH could take me. I sat in my room most of the time, because my Dad did not want to look at me. If anyone came over, I had to sit in my room and be very quiet so that they would not know that I was there. It was December, about a week after my fifteenth birthday, when they took me to Toledo. I was so scared and yet very anxious to get there. I knew that I would not have to 'hide' there. I would not have to hold my stomach in or sit in my room.

My first night there was a relief, as I could go to the big living room and watch television. We had one television at home and I was not allowed to sit in the living room, because someone might see me through the window. This was a luxury. When one of the girls asked when I was due, I thought that she said, *What do you do?* I told her I went to school. There were so many girls there, all different ages, some in high school, some in college and some like me still in grade school. One of the girls that I became friends with was only twelve and had lost her baby soon after she went to FCH, but her parents would not let her go home, because she was supposed to be overseas in a girls boarding school.

We were treated well. We had chores assigned to us weekly. I usually made breakfast. Everyone liked my oatmeal and coffee. I didn't drink coffee, but it gave me great pleasure to hear them say, *Linda Lou made the coffee this morning*. We went to school in the same building. One thing that stands out in my mind is that I had a favorite teacher in 5th grade. I think that he was the best teacher that I ever had. Imagine my shock and surprise when I saw him at FCH teaching a class. He never acknowledged me and I never let on that I knew him. I can tell you, it was a blessing just to see this kind gentleman every day. I had known him since 1st grade. I was in the same grade and the same school as his grandson – the Catholic school in a small town where everyone knew everyone.

My parents came to see me once in the six months that I was there. It was a disappointing visit. I was hoping to go to a nice place to eat, but instead they brought food from home and we ate in the car, parked a few blocks away from FCH. My Dad did have to come and get me one Friday evening, so that I could go to my dentist appointment. He brought me home very late, parked in the garage so that no one would see me. The next morning we left very early to drive the thirty miles to my dentist where I had my braces removed. As soon as that was done, he took me straight back to FCH. I was at home for maybe a total of nine hours. It had to be dark when I arrived home and we left before daybreak so that no one would see me.

Mom and Dad never called me. The reason was they did not want a Toledo 'phone number showing up on their 'phone bill. Someone that worked at the telephone office might see it and guess where I was. My letters from them were few and far between. They had to be sent to a family in Indiana and they would mail them to Toledo. The post office could not see my name on an envelope being sent to Toledo. When I wrote to them, it had to be read by the house mother and she would send it to Indiana and then it was sent on to my parents.

I did not have any sex education. When I was about ten my Mom showed me an ad for Kotex and asked if I knew what they were for. I thought I had some idea and I could see how embarrassed she was and so I just said that I knew. That was the extent of my sex education.

A social worker came to me a few times. She made me very nervous. She would ask about the father of the baby every time she came to see me. She told me that, if I loved my baby, I would give him up to a better home than I could provide. I was told that, if I kept him, I would be kicked out of my house with no place to live. I would have no money or any way to care for him.

She even went so far as to say the other children would not be allowed to play with him, because he would be a bastard. It would be hard for me to put him in school for the same reason. Every child had to have two parents. We were browbeaten into thinking we were 'bad girls' and we believed it. There was never a question of keeping our babies; we knew that we had to give them away. We were not prepared for childbirth. We had no idea of the pain.

When I went into labor I had to put a plastic sheet on the seat of the station wagon that took me to the hospital. I was put in a small labor room on a black gurney without a sheet. I was left alone for hours. I was not knocked out cold. I was groggy, but I can remember when my son was born. They told me it was a boy and he looked like me; he had my chin. The doctor brought him around to my face so that I could see him – *Oh My God, love at first sight*. I asked the Doctor what his name was, because I wanted to name the baby after him. His name was Doctor Philips. I didn't like that and so I named him Jeffery Lee. They asked if I was going to care for and feed my baby. Yes, I was. It seems like the delivery room was full of people, chock-full of people, but that might not be the case. I also remember it being very cold.

I had my son in May, 1965. My parents came to see my baby and fell in love with him. My Dad said, *You want to take him home don't you?* I said what I thought he wanted to hear. I said, *No. I do not deserve him.* After forty-five years I am still wondering what would have happened if I had said, *Yes. He is mine and he needs me.* Both my parents are gone now and so I will never know the answer to that.

I had to stay at the home until the end of June. I asked the social worker several times if I could see my baby. She told me, *No.* I had taken care of him every day while I was in the hospital and I missed him so much. Little did I know how much he was missing me.

We found each other in June, 2001.

My son was adopted twice. The second adoptive father hated him and called him 'the little bastard'. When the real children started to come along, he was pushed aside and was almost forgotten. His adoptive father was a drunk and a gambler. His adoptive mother had to take a job to support the family, but the adoptive father would come home on pay day and take her check after she went to sleep. They would then have to go to the adoptive mother's parents' home to eat and get money to pay the bills. My son told me that he was very close to his grandparents. His adoptive mother was adopted and in order to 'give something back', her Mom encouraged her to adopt a child, even though she didn't want to. Somehow her Mom won the fight and my son was adopted by a couple that did not want him.

There is much more to this story. Needless to say my son is an angry man and does not trust many people. I have my own opinion as to why he has cut off contact with me.

~~~~

Linda's daughter was born in the US in 1965

When I was twenty-two, I found out I was pregnant. My good, Catholic boyfriend of over a year suddenly didn't know how he felt about me. I was devastated. His priest persuaded me that adoption was the answer. I reluctantly agreed.

I had only a high school education, did not have a good relationship with my parents and had to quit my job. I went to a Catholic convent-style maternity home, with two old nuns as our 'house mothers' or whatever. (A constant reminder of our sins? We went to mass every day.) Everything was handled by Catholic Charities. We had good physical care but no counseling of any kind.

We were NEVER told we had any rights. (That would NEVER happen today.) The process was like a production line.

ADOPTION SEPARATION

When my daughter was born I was anesthetized and when I woke up she was already taken out of the room. I was advised not to see her, hold her or name her. I did all three. I was told to forget about it, put it behind me and get on with my life and that I could have other children.

After I was released from the hospital I returned to the Home, got my belongings and was sent home. I left with my mother. I think they wanted to get us away from the other girls as soon as possible. The day I went to court to sign the adoption papers was the most difficult day of my life. Not a day goes by that I don't regret my decision. A mother never forgets her child.

I later married the father. I know now I married him to try to make things right, but that's a whole other story. I had three sons. I never had another daughter. We later adopted two little girls from Asia. Almost five years ago my daughter found me. Little by little the memories started coming back. I started having health issues due to the stress and ended up in much-needed therapy.

Today, I feel I was cheated out of my child and my daughter feels like she was cheated out of her family. We are working on our relationship and have both agreed we want to be in each other's lives. She and my other children get along great. They and their spouses cannot get over the similarities between us. She and my husband (her father) are cordial to each other. I invite her to family functions and if she can make it she joins us. I've met her adoptive parents and they seemed to be all that I prayed for. That, in a nutshell, is my story.

It still bothers me when I see mothers with their young daughters. Interestingly, it bothers my daughter, too.

Mina's son was born in the US in 1965

July 25th, 1964, the 'BIG twenty-first' birthday, celebrated with my parents, at the *Top of the Sixes* restaurant, in Manhattan. I had a frozen daiquiri and felt so mature. On July 27th, I was surprised by a call from an old summer 'love', in Manhattan for a job interview, asking if I'd like to go out for dinner. Overjoyed, I accepted and looked forward to another memorable birthday event. Having irregular periods all my life, missing periods were not unusual. I was not experienced sexually and so I didn't think I could be pregnant. All we were doing was playing around, while parked at Plum Beach. Never being thin, I began to look heavier then usual. Was I pregnant? I had the 'rabbit test', but the rabbit lived. Was I surprised, on February 8th, 1965, to learn that I was SEVEN MONTHS pregnant.

Late in October, two days after my parents' thirty-first anniversary, my best friend and mentor, my Dad, had died. Life totally changed. Between my mother's sadness, student teaching in an all-girls high school, feeling awful, every morning and evening and seeing my body change, I was in denial. One of the students asked me, "When are you due?" Several of the girls were pregnant and so they could tell. My half-sister's doctor never really examined me, only did a finger blood test and put me on birth control pills. Finally, my mother was scared that I had a tumor and made an appointment for me with Doctor R, the doctor who had delivered me. In my mother's mind, there was my Dad, God and Doctor R.

I went alone and sat in the waiting room with other pregnant women. I was called, 'Mrs', like everyone else in the office. After being examined, I was told that I was perfectly healthy and SEVEN MONTHS pregnant. I went numb.

I was going to walk across the Grand Army Traffic Circle, a major traffic circle, without looking, so that I wouldn't have to deal with telling my mother this news. Doctor R called my

167

best friend, who picked me up in a cab and took me home. That evening we all went to a Chinese Restaurant and I told my mother that we had an appointment with Doctor R on Sunday morning. Sunday came. I sat on one side of the desk, my mother at the other end, near Doctor R. When he told her the news, she cried and screamed out, "Your father would turn over in his grave." Doctor R got up and tapped her on the chin. "She did nothing wrong. She is bringing a new life into the world", he said.

I grew up with two loving parents. Even though we were not rich, we had all the riches money can't buy. I was loved unconditionally, given every opportunity to explore, learn, grow and follow my dreams. How could I not give my child the same chance in life? This child deserved to be in a home, with two loving parents and know the feeling of belonging and unconditional love. In 1965, no matter how much I loved this life growing inside of me, it was impossible for me to raise this child as a single mother. I was going to be an Art Teacher, in the New York City system. The contract had a morals clause. There was no family support. Placing my child for adoption was the hardest decision I ever had to make in my life, but it was the only decision that was right for my child. I don't remember much after that except an attorney coming to the house to meet me. He offered money for everything — clothes, medical expenses and cash. All we accepted was medical care.

I continued to student teach, go to class and work as Art Editor for my college Year Book. I was becoming more withdrawn daily. Finally, it was decided that I take 'medical leave' from school for about a month. My assignments were delivered to me, with the galleys for the Year Book. No one saw me during the day. I was a prisoner in my home.

My best friend and her fiancé would pick me up late in the evening and drive to the other side of Brooklyn, so that we could have ice-cream at Jahn's. They tried to introduce me to one of his friends, but he didn't like the 'fat girl' and so that ended.

168

Then and now

April 1st, 1965 was the due date, but nothing happened. I kept going for visits, alone, being called 'Mrs' and was never told what to expect. Decisions were made to induce me. My mother and I took a cab to the hospital, which was the same one where I was born, at 6.45 am. Totally unprepared for what was going to happen, I was petrified. Then — I was dry shaven, given an enema, injected with sodium pentothal, put in a crib with bars and lined up like cars in traffic. Women were screaming from pain. All I wanted was to have this baby be healthy and then I could die. Doctor R's young partner, Dr. S, came to check me. My water broke in his face. The pain was intense. I remember looking at the clock. It was almost 9.00 am.

At 1.00 pm, I could see my toes, my mother and my best friend. My friend told me that I had a son, nine and a half pounds, twenty-three inches long, healthy and perfect. My mother was silent. I was given lunch, but couldn't eat.

A tiny nurse came to get me up off the bed. I fainted backwards. I was not on the maternity floor, but next to an old woman, dying of cancer. Later, a bigger, stronger nurse came to get me up and pushed me down on to a chair. I wanted to scream from the pain. I sat on a glove filled with ice to help with the pain. My blood pressure was so low that a group of interns came to see me as a learning specimen. A catheter was inserted, as they all watched. I was embarrassed and wanted to cry. Next was a laxative.

Several days later I went home from the hospital, emotionally and physically empty. The attorney held my son, all dressed in blue and wrapped in a blanket. I had to confirm his identity necklace before he could leave the hospital. He left. I cried.

People were told that I had hemorrhaged and was hospitalized to be stabilized. My Uncle Jack drove us home and asked in jest, "So where's the baby?" My mother almost fainted.

ADOPTION SEPARATION

My son was born on a Thursday and I returned to student teaching the following Thursday. Since I didn't breast feed, I leaked and wore pads. Six weeks later, I weighed a hundred and forty-three pounds, down from the hundred and eighty-nine pounds I weighed when I gave birth. I never weighed a hundred and forty-three pounds again. When I'd go out with my friends, my mother would say, "Have a good time, but don't get in trouble again." I graduated in June, 1965 with my class, but finished all my classes in summer school.

My mother became ill in August, 1965 and died of stomach cancer in April, 1966. I truly believe she never told anyone about my son. The day before she died, she came out of a coma and said she forgave me. I swore to myself that I would never be with a man again. Friends were getting married, having children and doing what all 'good girls' of the 60s did. I could not relate to little boys, but loved my two nieces, giving them the love that I would have given to my son. No one knew about my son until decades later. In one group therapy session, the counselor asked, "When are you going to stop living for your mother, start living your own life and forgive yourself?" That was a turning point for me.

When my son was six months old, I signed the final consent papers. I was told to say that the adopting couple were my cousins. I can't imagine what his adoptive parents went through during those six weeks months, knowing that I could have changed my mind and not signed the consent. The entire day is a blur in my memory, except that I read the papers before I signed them. I never forgot the name of his parents. I am Jewish. They are Jewish. His birthfather is Jewish. I was a college graduate and so were his adoptive parents.

I would not have chosen a couple that were not going to raise him in his birth religion. I dented my car as I left the garage, because I was in a daze.

Then and now

Not a day has gone by in the past forty-five years when I didn't think about my child. Whenever anything happened that would affect his age group, I worried about him. On his birthday, I'd started to smoke again. Holidays were lonely, even if I was with a group of people. When my nieces were old enough to date and understand, I told them about him, just in case they would ever meet in the dating world. My eldest niece made me cry telling me that she would have been there for me. She will be forty next year. The family all hope that the day will come when he is ready to meet me and them, face to face. Miracles do happen and so I haven't given up. It's ironic that my son is named after my maternal great-grandfather and paternal grandfather. His family name starts with the same initial as mine.

In a three year period I lost the three most important people in my life, my parents and my son. I was an orphan at twenty-two and on my own. It took decades for me to believe that it was safe to love openly and be loved, without loss. I picked men who were not available emotionally, so that when we parted, I was prepared. Finally, in the sixth decade of my life, I let someone into my heart, who is good to me and for me. We have a loving and productive relationship.

Forty-five years later my son is a successful businessman, as well as a loving husband and father to two beautiful children; a daughter who is almost five and a son, a clone of him, who is going to be a year old this fall. Just prior to his thirty-eighth birthday I found him through an Internet searcher. We have never had any personal contact. On his daughter's fourth birthday, he confirmed me as a 'friend' on the internet. He and his family live in my heart and prayers. To him I am just another 'friend' among many. I believe someday he will want to know me, as two adults who share a common bond and connect in person.

ADOPTION SEPARATION

Mirah's daughter was born in the US in 1967

1967 in America has been called 'The Summer of Love.' It marks the birth of my first child, my daughter, Alicia, born after I left an abusive marriage and was encouraged to place her for adoption.

My parents wanted me to 'put it all behind me' in order to start over – the whole 'mistake' (which included my unaccepted, inappropriate marriage and the child it produced). Social workers told me it was the unselfish, loving, caring, right thing to do and if I kept her we'd both wind up on welfare – unheard of for white, middle class girls! The longer I put off signing, the stronger the pressure became.

Forty-three years have passed. I have never forgotten. I have raised three children and still I grieve. It is the central point of my life, which has been devoted to revamping adoption practice in the United States. I have authored two books toward that end. During the ensuing four decades, I have been able to look back and see beyond my guilt and shame. When I do, I see a very frightened and vulnerable young woman facing a monumental, lifelong decision for herself and her daughter with no neutral counseling to explore options.

Looking back, I see a clear analogy. It was comparable to having a prosecutor telling me over and over to plead guilty to a crime I didn't commit, assuring me that to do so was 'best' and basically the only thing I could do. Yet not telling (as my own attorney would) the consequences, e.g. that I would have a lifelong criminal record. In the United States indigent people faced with a crime are granted a public defender. Not so for mothers about to sign away the life of their child!

Australia has changed their history of coercive adoption and one state has issued an apology for past practices. Here in the United States, because of the reduction in the numbers of women placing their children for adoption, as a result of birth control advances and more acceptance of single parenting, the pressure on unmarried expectant mothers has become more intense. In many ways adoption practices are worse now than they were in the 50s and 60s. The United States is the largest recipient nation of inter-country adoptions, adopting nearly half of all children from around the world. Most domestic adoptions in the United States are private and involve the adoptive parents and their attorney. If the relinquishing mother has any legal counsel, the adopters pay for it and the attorneys' job is to complete the adoption. An expectant mother chooses a new family for her child from photos and biographies and open adoption is offered, without full explanation of its unenforceability.

Women are encouraged not to reveal the name of the father and fathers' rights are often negated. In violation of the intent of laws that prohibit pre-birth contracts as baby buying and selling, the prospective adopters befriend mothers while they are alone and vulnerable and pay their living and medical expenses, creating a feeling of indebtedness. A mother is treated as a paid surrogate and encouraged to think of the baby she is carrying as belonging to others and not her own. In most cases, the prospective adopters are right there in the delivery room and allow the mother no time at all to rethink her decision in the light of meeting a real, live human being – her baby.

In forty-four of the fifty states, adoptees are currently not allowed access to their own original birth certificates; in all fifty states original mothers and fathers are forever denied the right to know the identity of their relinquished children.

As I learn of Australia continuing to move forward and apologize for past practices and the likelihood of an inquiry into these practices, I am filled with grief to live in a nation in which these unethical, immoral practices have become the accepted 'norm' and there is no national child adoption governing agency to oversee lax state adoptions laws. Demand for babies is allowed to create a supply and it's simply business as usual with little regulation in what some have called the wild west.

ADOPTION SEPARATION

Paula's son was born in the US in 1967

I will not know. This was the deal, really. *You may not know.* Not how your baby grows. Not how he'll be, next year. Not how or who he'll be in five years, ten, twenty-one – or ever.

This was the deal, take it or leave it. *Take your child or leave him.* With us, to do as we will.

No, *our very best – to do our very best.* People you've depended on say we are the very best agency here in this area and everyone has said and everything you've read agrees, this is the best, the very best choice to make; adoptive parents must be the best – they are carefully screened.

Everyone can love, indeed. As you have learned. Now you must believe this means this couple will love your child.

Prescreened.

As I am not – I, hardly helpless, no teen, a woman in my twenties, college-graduated, now adept already in the demonstrations and the street-fights, strong believer in the Struggle and the possibilities of love, nonviolence, hope, commitment – yet how can I, single, with no knowledge how to take care of a baby, no experience in childcare (yes, one summer counseling at children's camp, one afternoon of babysitting), no pre-proven evidence of parenting ability, raise such a child?

For he is a miracle, the most important baby, creature, being, person in the world, the universe. Yes, I have come to learn I love, to love myself, to deep awareness I love others and to love the many and seek to love everyone, yet who am I to – how can I dare – raise this miracle child? This child, carried through a hundred dangers and the demonstrations, nights of reaching through war's barricades, days struggling toward an end to war, this child of peace. How can I raise, so alone in this confrontation, this wondrous child, this fragile – yet strong – loving, tender, miracle child?

Then and now

The women cried. One brought the papers from the outer office, there in the agency, after I held him, my baby, you – so many papers they placed instead into my hands; I was to sign. Why were they being so overemotional, I wondered; after all, this was like any other office action, sign upon the dotted line. I did so.

Now you are here. You have returned to find me.

When he is ten, I shall come back here and find out how he's doing; by then, he'll be old enough. This will not intrude upon . . . What was I thinking? This was an insanity; this was denial. Did I really think it would be simple – that his whereabouts – he – would just be available when I decided to revisit the agency, come looking, find him? Did I not accept the law, or its realities?

Once I signed, I left the agency; I went back to the house where I was staying with the brilliant, vital woman of the Movement who had welcomed me and that night I went into the other, nearby house where he whom I had loved and who had braved and risked his very life against the war, now lived with his new love. And we would laugh together and there would be cake and gentle words. And I stepped into the kitchen, lifted a knife out of a drawer and halfway jabbed it in my chest, thinking, "Don't act so melodramatic," of course, before I let it fall.

The light of April streamed upon us as we marched, the greatest antiwar march ever, brilliant sunlight of the San Francisco streets upon us, for five miles, our banners and the new – the 'hippie' flowing clothes, uplifted god's-eyes, threads of silver and purple, rose-and-gold, the songs of love, our chanting – rose into the sky. And I shall live as if – as if I love this one or that, as if my love, reaching out, shall be returned, as if I shall return love reaching out to me, as if this one is there, is he and reaching shall find love, become love, be. And indeed, love did. Love reached and grew. In our world and in fact in me.

Only, you were gone. You were not there.

Ten years later – soon after I visited the agency and learned that they had no news of you beyond, "when the adoption was finalized, when he was one year old", but that what news they had was good, "very healthy, very active and responsive", "sensitive people who love the child very much" – I became again pregnant. My second son, I raised; he is the troubled one. You, however, are whole – or nearly whole. Sensitive, intelligent, responsible, careful for your adoptive parents, loving in reunion and careful, too, with me. Love reached out and grew. You were not here with me, yet you were there. And in your somewhere, which was your 'where I grew up' and your home – your own room, your toys, your house and neighborhood, your relatives, friends – you loved and reached out and grew.

I only know how much we cried when you, still a very young man, thin like a boy, found me; I only know we loved, we were like new-born and mama, healing. I know this means there had been loss, enormous loss, yet wholeness – wholeness, for we were each able to absorb and accept this openness, the vulnerability, in our reunion and not to flee; we were able to trust, hope, love. I know this means our separation for those years was necessary.

You are here. Love reached out and grew, reaches out and continues, widening, the ripples of joy.

~~~

Elizabeth's son was born in the US in 1968

I grew up in a family where everyone was beaten except me and I always wondered why. In some ways it was a good thing, of course and I suppose I was grateful for that, but in other ways it was a different kind of hell, observing and feeling left out somehow.

Then and now

Interestingly, my four older siblings turned out to be wonderfully responsible and incredibly good people and it was I who was the black sheep and who brought shame upon us all. I was the youngest of five children (six, but one sister was still-born) and the child of parents who did not seem to love each other at all throughout twenty-five years of marriage.

I deeply loved my mother, but I did not like her much of the time. I learned very early not to trust her. Her moods changed radically and one had to be ready to deal with whatever came up. She would threaten to kill herself often and was depressed and angry a lot. At times, the belt or a shoe would appear and people started getting hurt, including my father. I could never justify what she did, especially since she was a deeply religious person, who took her children to Sunday School every Sunday.

I worshipped and utterly adored my father, but because he owned his own business and worked late, I don't think any of us knew him well. I was afraid always that he would not like me. He was told to leave when I was in the second grade. My earliest wish was that they would find a way to get along.

I was fourteen in the summer of 1967. Already disconnected from most of my family through their respective marriages and my parents' messy divorce, I was longing for attention and love; this new boy fitted the bill. I would go to his house almost every day after school and listen to music, talk and then go to bed. I would always make it home before my mother did. Later, I found out that 1967 was known as the 'Summer of Love'. This could not have been more true for me.

Then, I got pregnant.

Mostly, I was in denial about my pregnancy, but I knew that I was in a lot of trouble. My mother finally found out and flew into a rage. At school the next day, my teacher noticed my injuries. I was placed in protective custody and my mother was called. When she told them her version of the events, they released me to her and told me that I deserved the beating. I am sure my mother omitted the fact that I was with child, as she was extremely ashamed of my condition, but they expelled me when they finally did find out. They told me not to return to school without a psychiatric evaluation.

I was sent away to a home for unwed mothers in Los Angeles on April 11th, 1968. The home was actually a good place for me. I was with other girls in my condition and happy away from my mother. No one could judge, as we had all done 'it'. We were all slated for giving up our children. That was the most tragic thing of all. A sense of utter futility and the resulting numbness surrounding that final day with our babies, permeated all of us.

There were regular, individual meetings held with all the girls. The social workers represented the Children's Home Society, the main adoption agency which was marketing our babies. They said we had options – that is, we could 'go on welfare for the rest of our lives', if we wanted to and thereby keep our babies. However, the message was very clear to all of us: if we wanted what was best for our babies, we would give them to couples who had what it took to raise a child properly, or more directly, if we loved our babies, we would sign.

I did not see a choice; I did not feel that I had one. Though I did not realize very much about what I was doing, I did know that I wanted my child to have something better than what I could give. I did believe that I was incapable and unworthy of being a mother. I did think that other people were better for my child. I never once dared to entertain the thought that I could keep my baby. It was an impossibility and that was all there was to it. My simple resolve still astounds me.

My closest brother died on May 27th. He had been sick with a cold and, within a month, it had turned into rheumatic fever. I stayed with my mother at my sister's house while all the arrangements for my brother's funeral were made. I was not allowed to attend, due to my mother's embarrassment of me and no doubt her own shame at my brother having died in her care.

I was taken back to the home and stayed there until my son was born. I had hardly seen my mother at all and we spoke neither of my brother, nor of my baby, except that she told me once that I dare not think I could bring him home. I signed the adoption papers all alone, holding my baby only once and taking the one picture that they offered, hoping secretly to find him again someday.

Once I turned sixteen, I quit school and got a job. I was numb and tired and I felt my life was over.

I became involved with a sometime friend of my brother. He was very abusive, telling me that I was 'damaged goods'. I believed him and so, at the age of sixteen, I married him. I became pregnant right away and had another son.

Somehow, being 'allowed' this time, to keep my baby, was overwhelmingly frightening to me. I could not admit that outwardly and didn't fully realize inwardly what was wrong with me either, until many years later. I know that I felt that I was not qualified to be my second child's mother. I was petrified that if anyone knew the truth, they would take him away also. I desperately needed to make it look as if I knew what I was doing and therefore could not ask anyone for advice, lest they discover that I was unfit. I was constantly afraid that the facade would all fall apart. My mind was clouded and my heart numb but I had not figured out why. A cycle of emotional neglect began.

My husband was an alcoholic. He beat me and insulted me daily. I wanted nothing more than to be away from him. Finally, when my son was one year old, I got free.

I was seventeen, living alone, had had two children and had been married and divorced already. If boys my age were interested, they could not bring me home to meet their parents. I had only one friend.

179

I then met a man, twenty-two years older, whom I later married – at age eighteen. He was not much better, but because he liked my son, I thought it would work. I felt I was in love, but more importantly, I thought he would stay with me.

Within a year, at age nineteen, I had a daughter and the very next day, had my tubes tied. I had realized that I kept picking unsuitable men. I had not discussed this decision with anyone. My marriage ended within five years.

At this point, I was twenty-three with two children and no child support, no husband and no education. I was on welfare, just as 'they' had predicted and I was devastated. I tried odd jobs – working in bars, working as a dancer, working in restaurants, but it was not work that I could be proud of. My siblings were all upstanding citizens with good professions and I wanted better for my children.

I realized that I had been drifting since my first pregnancy. That was where my life had gone wrong. I thought of my first child every day, longing to know how he was, at least. I felt that I had done the wrong thing giving him away. I felt guilty though, because I had been told to forget. I was told to keep it a secret. It was a deep conflict within me. Daily, the reality of my failures hung over my head, as I faced impossible odds now, with my two other children.

My two small children were looking to me for answers, that I only wished I could give them. Though my relationship with my daughter was very positive, I was often being abusive to my son; yelling, excessive spanking, name-calling. I was still angry at his father for his failures, angry at myself for mine, even angry at my son for being the precocious child that he was. There were times that I thought it was making him stronger, as the beatings had done for my siblings. I thought I was weak because I had not been beaten in my formative years. I wanted my son to be better and stronger than me.

Then and now

Like me, my daughter was traumatized as a witness to abuse – and still remembers. Though I actively sought help in parenting classes and Parents Anonymous, it was not until he was ten that the abusive cycle with my son was broken.

At one point, I had asked my sister and brother-in-law to take my two children for a few months. My husband was in trouble with the law and we needed to build his defense case. My sister was a perfect mother, in my way of thinking and I wanted my children to have that – something I could not give them. I was even more aware then, of my failures.

After my second divorce, my ex-husband began kidnapping our daughter. Though he eventually would return her, it happened so much that she was pulling her hair out, nervously and my son was devastated. I had asked my mother if we could come and live with her and she had refused. I tried hiding my daughter, along with my son, in a foster home and then he found her there too. I decided that if my ex-husband's brother and sister-in-law raised her, she would have the peace and stability she deserved. The biggest motivation was that I knew he would not steal her from them.

I moved with my son to Arizona after the signing of my daughter's adoption papers – the second time that I had relinquished a child – but, this time at least, I knew where she was and who was raising her.

I had started drinking. I grew to appreciate the joys of oblivion. It was now solidly obvious that I was a bad mother and I actually told this to my only remaining son. I spent the next few years trying to make things look normal still, but never quite succeeded. My son got into trouble with the law and was sent to an institution at age eleven. He was released at fourteen, not wanting to live with me and began being abusive to me, both physically and verbally. Finally, he ran away to live with ex-relatives in California, coming home only once for a year when he was eighteen.

ADOPTION SEPARATION

I met my daughter again when she was fifteen. I had agreed not to visit, nor to communicate with her. The meeting was magical for me. I had kept her so close in my heart, that it felt like we had never been apart somehow, though it had been twelve years.

My life has been mostly alone, at least for major events. About twenty years ago, I reconnected with my first child's birthfather and lived with him for ten years, hoping to salvage something of my life and also to meet our son one day. I had begun the process of searching on the day our son would have turned twenty-one.

Eventually, as it turned out, we met our son but he was not happy to have been found. It was a huge fantasy-buster to experience his seeming reluctance. Still it is amazing each time I am in his presence.

Also, I stopped having nightmares involving child-sized coffins. I hadn't connected the two until later realizing that the dreams had not returned.

My second son does not acknowledge me as his mother. My daughter's and my relationship is strained. I do not blame them, mostly, as they all have valid reasons, but I wish that, as adults, we could all be working on having a relationship in the present. I admit, I am not good at this either; there is a lot of fear. I am very willing though and I love all of them, dearly.

A few years ago, my first son's birthfather and I realized we did not want the same things, but I will always love him and we keep in touch, almost daily. I believe we really care about each other. I believe my life would have been so different had I been allowed to keep my first child. I think that, with help, I could have been a decent mother to him. I would have grown into the role and learned along the way. I am against unnecessary adoptions of the sort that I feel I was a victim of. I call them 'permanent solutions for temporary problems.' I have known young girls who raised their child and it worked out well, without the fragmentation of such terrible loss. I know of others who had difficulty with being young mothers, but so do adoptive parents. They are not perfect either.

It took a dear friend five years to convince me that I was smart enough to attempt getting my High School Diploma, but I did it at age twenty-eight, finally. With this new confidence, I both worked and attended school for many years, earning a Master's Degree, finally at age forty-eight. It turns out, ironically, that I have somewhat of a gift for working with children. As a teacher now, for twenty-eight years, I go about my day in the classroom often thinking of my own young children and how simple things could have been, had there been proper guidance and given time.

I 'came out' publically as a birth mother when I met my first son. Not keeping so many secrets is freeing, but unfortunately, it seems to have made some people around me very uncomfortable. Some see no problem with adoption, though they would tell you adamantly that they could never give up a child themselves. This always perplexes me about their stance, since someone has to give up a child to make adoption possible.

Therapy has helped but I will always have a massive void. I never will be normal. There is no recovery, no forgetting, no forgiving – of or for myself.

None of this needed to happen, I believe.

~~~~

Kathy's son was born in the US in 1968

I grew up in a rural farming community in the middle of the United States. My boyfriend and I were both aged seventeen and juniors in high school when I became pregnant, on the very first time we had sex in the summer of 1967.

ADOPTION SEPARATION

I was not allowed to attend my senior year at the school we had been attending. I was sent off to an 'Unwed Mother's Home' about two hours away.

There were fifteen pregnant girls residing at this two storey brick dormitory building. My parents had chosen a place that was of the same Christian faith base as the church our family attended. That way my baby would be adopted to a couple who attended the same type of church we attended.

The Home had us continue our school studies. I spoke to a social worker weekly and I wanted my boyfriend to marry me and that way we could keep our baby. That is what society believed back then; if a baby didn't have a mother and a father then, as an unwed mother, I shouldn't keep the baby. My baby would have been teased and called a 'bastard' as he grew up if I wasn't married. I begged my boyfriend to marry me, but he would have nothing to do with it. I remember I was so nervous during my stay in the home that my fingers itched and broke out in a rash. This was a very stressful time.

The small community that I came from was around two thousand people and I felt everyone in the community knew that I was pregnant and I was made to feel like a slut, a sinner and a loose girl. I lived a life of shame and this has affected me my entire life.

I delivered my baby at thirty-one weeks. I was so frightened not knowing what to expect. A lady from the home took me to the hospital. I had an epidural that actually failed and caused back pain from that day until now. Again I felt I 'deserved' the punishment of that procedure that went wrong. The nurse in the delivery room allowed me to see my baby son for about ten seconds, as she held him in a white sheet that draped over him. I was never allowed to hold my baby and I didn't even know I could, because no one counseled me on what I was or wasn't allowed to do with my baby.

Then and now

I found out thirty-six years later that a friend of mine from the Home held her baby many times and it made me really sad and angry that I didn't have that same opportunity. I know now my son and I would have been healthier if we could have had that time together.

I returned to my home town by the first of February, 1968 and went through the graduation ceremonies with my classmates that May. The administration at my high school put me by myself in a little room off the principal's office to finish my studies and again I felt ostracized and guilty. No one talked about my baby. There was no one insightful enough to say they were sorry for my loss. I just felt like I deserved all the punishment that came my way because I had done such a horrible thing by getting pregnant.

The father of my baby and I never dated again and never spoke about the whole incident after I came back to my high school. However he did come to the unwed mother's home once to visit me.

I did marry, in 1972, but within the first month of our marriage my new husband tried to hit me and yelled at me with such anger that he spat on me. I wanted so badly to run out the door and never come back but I couldn't; there was no place for me to go. The reason I had to stay in this tragic marriage is because I could not bring more shame upon my family with a baby out of wedlock followed by a divorce. That would have been just more than I could bear and so I stayed. Even though I knew the marriage was not a healthy one to have children in, I felt that if I didn't have children with this man, I would never have children and so we had a son and a daughter.

My controlling husband was never open to the thought of me trying to find the son that I lost to adoption. It took my daughter, at age twenty-four, searching on the internet who found her brother, my son. That was in 2004 when he was thirty-six. That reunion is what caused me to find Evelyn Robinson, because I knew I was mentally strong, but the emotions I was going through with the reunion were taking me to places I didn't know existed. I thank God for Evelyn and the work she has done to help mothers like me.

My adopted son and I communicated for about five years and now I have not heard from him in over eighteen months, but we are at peace. He is working on his marriage and family. The reunion with the son I lost did eventually lead me to divorce my controlling husband, after being married for thirty-five years. We have been divorced three and a half years now.

My precious daughter this summer, 2010, convinced me that it was time that I 'move on' in my life and branch out to find a new relationship. I signed up on one of the internet sites, but I told my daughter that I wanted to try to find this one first love that I had in high school and college before I started dating other men.

What I am about to say still has me in shock. This special boyfriend dated me before and after I came back to my high school from the unwed mother's home and we were each other's first love. He has now been found. We communicated by e-mail for about four months. As I am writing this to Evelyn today, I want you to know that after not seeing this wonderful man for forty years, I flew to meet him and we have rekindled our first love. He proposed during our reunion and we are living this 'fairy tale' that has come true. I have never been happier in my life.

~~~~

Linda's son was born in the US in 1969

My story begins back in 1950, when I was born to a mother who felt it was best to place me for adoption. It was a very difficult decision for her, but her husband made it clear that he didn't want her to take me home, because I was not his.

Then and now

She had met my birth father in Illinois during a separation from her husband and then got back with him. She was from Wisconsin, but I was born, adopted and raised in Minnesota. She gave me the best gift, since she loved him too much to leave him; she got me away from an abusive alcoholic, who would have abused me terribly, knowing his history.

I was six months old when placed with my adoptive parents. A few months later the adoption agency saw that there were problems and contemplated taking me back. They decided to leave me there, because my adoptive parents were going to fight for me and they had the finances to win. My adoptive mother was raised in a dysfunctional family and abused by her sister. She never knew what love was and although extremely religious, she was not a very nice person and became abusive to us as we grew into our teens.

My first true love was so good to me, but my parents wouldn't accept him, even after I became pregnant at the age of sixteen. They threatened to send me to a girls reform school. They beat me up and I ended up miscarrying the baby, when I was three months along.

It was devastating to both of us and my parents were so mean to him that he finally walked away from our relationship; I was heartbroken.

Life went on, I had a few more boyfriends, but then I met the one who would be a huge mistake. I was going to break it off, but we got together for New Year's Eve and one thing led to another. I found out three months later that he had purposely got me pregnant so that I would have to marry him. He knew how I felt about adoption and knew I would choose him instead of giving up my child for adoption, which were the only choices back then. If abortion had been legal, I probably wouldn't be writing this story.

We were married and, after several beatings, we ended up divorced two years to the day from the date we married. My son was born six weeks prematurely by caesarean section. He was very sick and I didn't get to be near him for several days after his birth. I finally got to take him home when he was eighteen days old and I loved him so much. We were so poor, but I did the best I could. My ex-husband was worthless and was becoming mentally ill. My adoptive parents were no help; they said that I had made my bed and so I should lie in it.

I finally got away from the marriage, but life as a single mother in the early 1970s, living on welfare, was a terrible way of life.

As the years went by, I found myself feeling more and more worthless. I loved my son so much, but I knew that I wasn't giving him all that he needed to become the man I knew he could be some day. After asking all of the relatives I thought could take him until I could get on my feet and get a job that paid enough to raise him and getting no support or help of any kind, I finally gave up. I called the agency that I had been adopted through and went in, telling them that I thought the best thing for my son would be having two parents who could give him more than I could. They saw my perfect little boy, who was raised with so much love and pushed one family in particular, who I later learned were friends of a Social Worker who worked at the agency. They wanted an older boy and he was a good match, in the agency's eyes.

The day came when my five year old son would meet the people who might be his new parents. I had to drop him off at the agency and go back home. He was supposed to come home for a night or two before the move and so I knew I would have more time with him. Around 4.00 pm the social worker brought him back to me, but then started saying how wonderful the meeting had gone and since they lived so far away they wanted to take him that night. She felt it was best and wouldn't even allow him to ride with me to the agency parking lot, where I dropped off all of his things and had to hug him good bye. I was so distraught and totally depressed that I allowed her to manipulate me into doing the wrong thing and the memory still haunts me after thirty-five years.

The agency made a mistake and I was given the address where my son had gone. I learned that they did not live far away. It was only forty-three miles from me. After a few years had gone by and I was not getting the updates and openness the agency had promised me, I contacted the adoptive parents directly.

They got a friend who was their attorney to speak with me. During the meeting with him, I learned that the parents were Jewish rather than Protestant, which I had asked for. I also learned that the mother was not at home, as I was told and that they were never told of the promise made to me for communication.

I kept my cool and after speaking a while I think he decided that I was a good person, because the communication between the adoptive parents and me became very satisfying for us both. So much so that they gave him a letter from me when he was nineteen, so that we could reconnect. They sent a letter and photograph once a year. It saved my life knowing that he was all right and in the end they gave their blessing to him to meet with me again.

Our reunion has worked out. There was a time when his son was five years old that he wanted to punish me, but we got through it and seem to have a healthy, loving relationship.

His children call me Grandma just like the others. I am forgotten more than the other grandparents, but I can't expect the time the others get. At least when we are together we really enjoy each other and that counts more than anything. I love my son and never stopped loving him. At least his parents told him the truth so that he always knew I gave him up because I loved him so much and he needed more than love could provide.

I've worked on my self esteem, grief and guilt issues and pretty much have accepted my life and hope that my son has found the healing our reunion has given me. We talk about how adoption has affected both of us.

Reunion with my birth families was very healing for me and I had a wonderful relationship with my birth mother for twenty-three years before she passed on. It's too bad the law prevented us from knowing each other before I placed my son for adoption. She would have helped me, no questions asked, as her love was unconditional.

~~~~

Cathy's daughter was born in the US in 1970

I was twenty-one.

A trip to Washington to visit my college boyfriend of more than three years. He'd graduated almost two years before.

Then, fear, worry, was I? Distraction, anxiety, doctor, shots, revisit. Yes, I was.

School, crying, praying, worry, fear, denial, inward pulling, no word from boyfriend.

We had, without a fight, broken up. I refused to call. I waited to see, did he care at all? Would he ever call me again?

No.

Weeks go by, then months. I pack and leave for home. I know I won't return.

Silence. Denial. The truth and its consequences are beyond imagining. The terrible thought of 'telling' – just shut down and it isn't happening.

If I weren't here, maybe...I'd save so many people misery and shame. I thought I was going crazy. Paralyzed with terror, I didn't have any idea how to help myself.

I remember.

My mother was away – finally a girl trip with friends. I had to tell my father. .... But how? I had seven younger brothers and sisters. Such very good parents; earnest, straightforward and decent, hardworking, honorable and steadfast – with expectations. How does one who never has, open her mouth to speak the truth about herself and how does he hear those most shocking words. Finally, defeated, I offered up my secret shame. "I have to go to a home."

"Stop crying. I'll make you breakfast."

I remember.

But inwardly, I never stopped crying.

My mother returns and, because I can't, my father tells her. Mother: "Haven't I told you the woman always pays?" Well, … No. "You must call him. Are you sure there is no one else?"

I do. I am. He comes from far away. He is loving and concerned. He says he can tell; I'm fuller. I make no demands. But I'm afraid. He says he'll leave and then send for me. How could I not have more forcefully advocated for myself? I couldn't see the future. I couldn't know that this was just the beginning of a treacherous journey – a journey with a dreadful ending.

My father makes plans – just in case – Catholic Charities, far away. I'm to be a nanny. I tell the social worker, "I'm not staying here. I'm getting married." "Oh? To whom? Where is he?" she said coldly. That one cruel moment was when I really got it.

Then the letter: "I used to love you then, but not now. I thought you were pure, but I found out you weren't ..." I threw the letter away, turned and faced my fate. The man I had loved threw us away, our baby and me. I never heard from him again.

One house with children, then another with a woman who said her own daughter would never, ever, find herself 'like you'. Then the Irish woman, whose husband had a lobotomy. She needed the money. She was kind, but I was miserable; so unhappy and unable to express anything about myself, about why I felt so desperate, lost and afraid. I just got on that treadmill to nowhere, brainwashed. This was the only path I'd ever heard of.

I remember.

ADOPTION SEPARATION

The doctors and nurses, disgusted. Once, when I was wearing a sort of girdle, a doctor said, "What are these lines? Why don't you grow up and face reality?" He was abrupt and indifferent. I was not a person of interest to him.

I knew what was coming, but how could I know the lifelong sadness I'd feel? I only thought about us as one, my baby and me. She was safe and while we were together I knew just where she was. But I never spoke of my love for her. I never once mentioned out loud how sad and abandoned I felt. Only by myself and late at night, I'd let the truth in. I just went with the program. This is what one did. Hide. Deny. Give away.

Long lonely months lumbered by.

Then waiting, waiting, due date, then past one week, then two, then three. My mother comes and takes me to a motel. Early in the morning, I think I must go to the hospital. Finally. Shaved, manhandled, shot up with twilight sleep, waking, being in a crib/cage and begging someone who never looked up, to help me. Then birth and the gathering of loose abdomen and groaning with pain to push out afterbirth. Then infection set in. She had been so big and perfect, so ripe, so ready, she blasted out of me.

And yes, I saw my baby. She was gorgeously fat and beautiful. Her dimpled face is etched in my memory. I thought she'd be blonde with blue eyes. They took her, saying it would be better not to see her at all. My mother on leaving said, "This is not a good way to have a baby." I was completely devastated.

I remember.

My baby left, I stayed, what was left of me. Just a shell. Then my father came to free me and to Catholic Charities to sign surrender papers; its own special hell. "Do you want your father to come in with you?" "No." Why kill him more? I'm already dead.

Now I see it was to witness my signature, to protect them. Then walking to the car, crying: "Why are you crying?" "Because it's just so sad." "Yes it is. It is the saddest thing in the world."

Then and now

After twenty-seven years of unspoken misery, a social worker calls me; someone wants to contact me. I can't. I have young children. I'm too afraid. I don't know how to out myself. Without understanding why, I know I cannot stay alive and go through this. I'm deranged with fear. Choking, I tell my father. He says, "Do not open that door." I shut down and I turn that phantom away. Or am I the phantom?

How was I to know how much pain my fear and inability to respond caused her? I didn't know she missed me. I didn't know she longed to know me. I'd been told it was just curiosity. Curiosity could kill a person. Silent, deep fearful grief sets in and more passage of time. I am desperate for her, but unable to help myself.

Nothing can explain my profound unhappiness, my fear and grief. I can't open my mouth to find help. I need help desperately.

Then thirty-five years have passed, without uttering a word about her. One day, July 12th, 2006, 2.00 pm to be exact, the phone rang – it was she, a sweet and gentle voice – my lost daughter. Could I talk? Did a day in November, 1970 mean anything to me? Did any other moment in time really define me? She'd hired a private investigator to find me.

Such shocking joy. I felt as though a knife had been pulled out of my heart. Such bravery, too. But she's a girl with a lot of courage.

I remember.

Then the terrible healing began. How was she able to withstand so much pounding of story? So many tears being unleashed. On and on and over and over. She held my hand – across a long distance.

I'm better. She's lovely, gentle and patient. My daughter. She has been more the mother to the injured bird. I am lucky, I have this chance. I'm taking it.

193

There is more understanding now about 'us', we surrendering mothers. More acknowledgment of how cruel that time was. I've benefited from other people's stories, their courage and generosity in 'telling', their compassion in listening to me. I replace painful memories with knowing this real and wonderful girl. How helpful that is.

My soul is filling. I can see now how much I hurt myself by burying my grief. How unnecessary that self punishment was.

Now I will speak the truth, to honor so many others, to heal myself, to know and love her, my daughter and to show empathy toward myself too, to see the experience as a rough one – and especially to be a witness to the suffering of others. It's not nothing to give away your baby.

I am becoming a whole person and, though it's late, perhaps I can be a better mother to my raised children who never really got all of me. Because now I have her.

But I will never forget.

~~~

Jim's son was born in the US in 1970

Clint is the name of my son who was put up for adoption over forty years ago. Adoption has had much unnecessary pain and suffering associated with it. I am very proud of Clint today, but my feelings weren't always pride.

Clint was born in 1970 at a time when single parenting was not the norm. I was seventeen and not a Christian. Unplanned pregnancy in the 1950s – 1970s was a big, bad deal!

Today, people don't even blink at the notion of teen parenting. Back in those days, you didn't talk about it, you hung your head in shame and embarrassment and if you were an Anglo (White), very often the baby was put up for adoption.

Then and now

The birthmother was fifteen, I believe, at the time and we had been in a secret relationship for a couple of years. Although I used birth control, the pregnancy was my fault, since I grew up in a culture where it was masculine to be sexually active before marriage. I got that message from my father as well as my older brother, whom I very much respected then, as I do today.

The night I found out the birthmother was pregnant was several months after we had broken up. It was one of the worst nights of my life. When I heard the news, the dam broke and I cried in the knowledge that I had hurt the birthmother in ways I could never comprehend, disappointed my parents and basically wrecked my life, big time. I had never felt such shame! I immediately told my parents. My parents, as well as the birthmother's parents, were on rocky ground. Divorce hit both families in the years right after the surrender for adoption.

My mother was empathetic, but my father was not. My family never mentioned the baby after he was born and my father fled our family, within a year or two.

My parents directed me to help out with the medical costs. At this tragic time, I was in junior college, since I had graduated from high school in three years. I began working full time and going to college full time and going crazy part time. It was a few years later when I went nuts, full time. When I got paid from my job, I would go by the birthmother's house and drop off money. We never talked about the pregnancy or birth. Coming from a house where people did not talk about feelings, that was all right with me. I decided to bury my feelings of pain, loss, separation and confusion under a mountain of marijuana and later lines of powdered cocaine. Drinking to medicate myself became a frequent pastime for me and anyone who chose to spend time with me.

You can only hold the lid on so long. Clint, as I was later to learn his name, was never too far from the surface. When I watched a movie about babies, birth or abandonment, the tears would easily flow. I knew something was wrong with me, but I couldn't put it into words. I did not learn about grief in my primary family. As time progressed, I did well in college, became a counselor and was successful in the early years of my career in the helping profession. There were always the haunting questions. What happened to the baby? Is he/she OK? What kind of person am I to have a child, but take such limited responsibility? Should I be a counselor when I have some of these issues floating around in my psyche?

When I was in graduate school, my wife of many years got pregnant. She was not the birthmother. The baby was not planned and so I was very scared. There were problems in my marriage and so I sought marital counseling from a clinical social worker while I was getting my master's degree in social work.

Early in the sessions, the notion of loss was introduced and I began a serious grief process. It was hard work, but it was all good stuff! It prepared me appropriately for parenthood and my second son was born in 1980, ten years after Clint. I decided that the time had come to talk to the birthmother of my son.

The meeting with Clint's mom went well. We were amicable and she shared with me that Clint (not his name given at birth) had been put up for adoption. She had gone to a residential program for pregnant teenagers in San Diego and it was 'game over', so to speak. Little did I know we were only in the first half! Grief work and the truth are helpful, but one thing leads to another. I had some peace with the birthmother, but life's losses don't neatly go into boxes up on the shelf of the dark closet.

Alcohol and drugs were losing their appeal and power and I began to work on my chemical dependency. I have been clean and sometimes serene for the past twenty-four years. Through counseling, I realized that my surrendered son was important to me and, to become whole, somehow and some way, I had to deal with him. I didn't know what to do, but if I wanted to face him someday, I needed to be a person worthy of meeting.

Through my work, I contributed to a booklet on coping with pregnancy loss or child death. Because of the book and my experience, I became an authority on grief counseling. At one conference, as a panel member, I mentioned that I had experienced an adoption loss. During the break, a woman told me that she was a birthmother and a member of a national organization called CUB (Concerned United Birthparents). She shared with me how she had found her child with the help of CUB. I went home, called CUB in Massachusetts and found a meeting in San Diego to attend. The meeting began a long relationship that led me to finding my son.

The first meeting I attended, as I began to share my story and my tears, I looked up and most of the people in the room were sharing in my grief. I saw tears on many faces and it was the first time I didn't feel alone with my grief. It was wonderful! It also established extreme faith in the support group model and a long time love for my sisters in CUB.

I commuted the two hours and attended monthly meetings for a few years before I got up the courage to search for my son. The first step was to send a letter to social services and ask for 'non-identifying' information. This was information about the adoptive family, but no names, places or specifics. At this time, I got a picture of Clint at birth! For the first time, I felt like what I had done sixteen years ago wasn't a bad thing. Being a part of creating life is always a good thing. For the first time, I felt self esteem about a mistake that had occurred. I was rewarded for my efforts to seek information.

The adoption system is often based on the notion that children are commodities and the owners (adoptive parents) have all the rights. This has been reinforced by the court system and a series of laws, honed by lawyers. Most adoptions require lawyers and so the bent system of social welfare has been molded by the hands of adoptive parents, lawyers and social workers, all of whom have never paid much attention to those on whose needs the system should be based. There are few states in which adopted people have the right to their original birth certificates.

Organizations continue advocacy and education and the bureaucratic change is as slow as molasses; if that fast. Fortunately, adoptive parents are more open and birthparents are becoming more assertive. Too often the adoptive parents just want to get the baby and for the birthparents to disappear. The lawyers want their big fat fees and the social workers are just co-dependants who want to please people with power to leave them alone.

When Clint turned seventeen, I found him living with his adoptive parents about three thousand miles away. CUB helped me to do the search and, whenever possible, I did most of it myself.

My reunion experience was almost ideal. Clint's adoptive mother was an adoptee and she knew the pain of not knowing her 'herstory'. She was open to a meeting, as was his adoptive father. We have been friends for years and, after reunion, I visited them a few times and even had Clint come out to brutally hot Imperial Valley and take a summer job at a bank where my wife worked. He was a business major in college and we had great visits.

When I found Clint, my CUB sisters encouraged me to involve the birthmother in the process. Being a person who can harbor a multitude of negative emotions, it was good that I got wise counsel. I did and she and I got along fine. All that was back in the late 1980s. As I write this now, in 2010, the skin on my face is peeling from the sunburn from the beautiful beaches of San Diego.

Clint and his seventeen year old daughter came out for a little vacation and we bade farewell yesterday. It was great to hold my granddaughter and know that we are beginning a much closer relationship, now that she is entering adulthood. Clint is a fine man and a fun person to spend time with. He is still too far away in distance, but always close at heart.

Then and now

My faith and love took me farther than I had thought possible and my love deepened more than I would have ever imagined.

~~~~

Ruth's son was born in the US in 1972

As I look at a fading photograph, I have the same queasy feeling in my stomach that I had then. My sweet boyfriend and I are standing under the mistletoe, our expressions masked. I am four months' pregnant. We are so scared. Protectively we wrap our arms around my little belly. I have been hiding the pregnancy, constantly afraid. I am sixteen years old; it is 1971.

My boyfriend wanted to marry me, but his affluent parents refused; they threatened to cut him off if we did. It's not that we are afraid of losing money, but what can we do on our own? They wanted us to break up. He steadfastly stayed with me, honorably and lovingly offering comfort.

We follow the logical line of each 'choice': If...we married and he quit school to support us, he would be drafted. We were afraid going to Vietnam would be a death sentence. I wouldn't let him do that.

If...we brought the baby to be raised at my house? My alcoholic father was kind, but my mother repeatedly and randomly beat him and me. She was terrifying; I know now she was mentally ill. She beat me throughout my childhood. If I tried to intervene as she screamed and hit my father, I was slapped until I fell to the floor and then kicked. She insisted my father's drinking was the problem; we had to hide him or risk losing the house and no one must know about our family matters. I lived in constant fear, but put on a front of normalcy; it was all I had. I trusted no one.

199

ADOPTION SEPARATION

Once they knew I was pregnant, no one else came forward to offer us aid, to take in our baby and me, to offer any alternatives or any wisdom.

If I had left with the baby...Where would I go? Being without the protection of some family, any family, was terrifying. The welfare families I saw were frightening. The adults drank and swore; the kids were mean or cowered. They were filthy, deceitful and wore ragged, smelly clothes. I couldn't imagine what kind of job I could get, without a high school diploma and who would take care of the baby while I worked? A girl with a baby cannot go back to high school.

I was sent to a 'home' for unwed mothers. The nuns there told me: wanting to keep our child was selfish, we were greedy for wanting to see each other, our baby would be better off with two respected, adult parents who were ready to have a child, we didn't deserve a child, if I really loved my baby, I would want what's 'best' for him, his adoptive parents had more education, money, a peaceful home, a respected, solid job, we were not worthy of respect, we were just kids, I had made a 'mistake' that could be 'fixed', I could have more babies later and I would go back to being a carefree teen and forget. I didn't believe the nuns.

I had no crystal ball to see into the future, but I knew there were no alternatives. I knew in my heart, ***all we have is love***, but no life skills and no one to turn to.

What other 'choice'? I had a friend who was adopted and her parents were terrific, the sweetest most loving parents I knew...We tried to think about adoption, how would it feel to lose our baby? We thought of keeping him safe; protecting him from our families. I have an image of being in a burning building with one exit, one second to decide who will be saved. We decide to save our son, even if it means tearing out our hearts, bleeding and still beating from our chests. If he were adopted, he would be spared. We trusted he would have a happy life and he would have a wonderful family like my friend's. I pictured him going to a perfect, beautiful family – a loving, kind mother who embraces her children, a sweet dad who laughs and reads stories, a family surrounded by light, happiness and peace.

My feeling about adoption was a 'going to', rather than a 'giving away'. I wished I could go there too.

The 'home' for unwed mothers is a respite from my house, but I feel numb. I feel I am reading about my life in a book; it all feels unreal.

When labor began, the nun on duty called a cab. In a strange city, in the middle of the night, she was going to send a frightened seventeen year old in labor *alone* to the hospital, but one of the older girls got in the cab with me, over the nun's protests. Alone, I was admitted, isolated in a room. I woke from a fog of drugs to find my monstrous mother holding my hand, weeping. I was disgusted and repulsed. In my leaden delirium it took all my strength to pull my hand away. I wanted to scream, but the sound was choked in my throat. I fought the drugs and the feeling of powerlessness. I must stay aware, must take care of my baby, don't want to lose him …

My young doctor was compassionate, gentle and kind. I trusted her and melted into her care. It was the first time I had ever met her.

I was only allowed to hold him for a little while in the hospital. With other new mothers, the nurses cooed and guided. With me, they said little, were brisk, plopped him in my arms, walked away with a judgmental 'harrumph'. One nurse lectured me on having had sex before marriage, while I sobbed and choked on my lunch. When they presented me with a medical release form, I understood that I was vastly inadequate as a mother and that I would not be able to take care of any emergency or illness with him. I would have signed anything to keep him safe.

Throughout my pregnancy I never felt shamed, though I felt adults thrusting it at me. The shame belonged to the people who did not tell us about sex (the rhythm method doesn't work).

Shame belonged to our families, community and church that did not help us and support us. Our son came from our love and commitment and had a God-given right to be loved and supported by his parents. We were thwarted in all our efforts; punished and ridiculed.

My son was perfect and I adored him. I can still smell his sweet new-baby scent; feel his miraculous warm weight in my arms. My boyfriend was not allowed to see him or me in the hospital. The hospital would not put the name we chose on his birth certificate, or, outrageously, his father's name and two years were added to my age. In the 'home' I was only allowed to see him through a window for fifteen minutes a day. I left the hospital with my breasts leaking milk, aching, with empty arms, shaking. *I didn't know how I could live another day.* My head hurt, I was weak in the knees and I could barely eat. At night I folded a blanket in the shape of my baby and rocked, as I wept in the darkness.

I could not stand the thought of not being with him forever, of not having him in my life.

I prayed for a miracle but no miracle came. I felt that the whole world turned against us. It took me months to gather the strength to sign the papers that would relinquish him to his adoptive parents.

The nuns' predictions didn't come true. I didn't return whole-heartedly to teen life and forget. I was distracted and part of my heart was forever with my baby. What was he doing? I longed to hold him, my chest ached, my heart raced, sometimes I could barely breathe. The life of my friends seemed shallow and pointless. The teachers punished me. My 'counselor' was surprised that I wanted to apply to college. I was not offered counseling from the 'home'. My 'caseworker' came once and asked my mother how I was doing. She said I was fine, put on a show of how disappointing I had been and how she had sadly endured it all.

Then and now

No one in the family ever spoke to me about my experience. I mourned in solitude.

Back home with my parents...After one thunderous fight, I came out of hiding and found my father pacing, smoking with a glassy-eyed stare. My mother had stabbed him twice in the arm; his blood was dripping down. He was in shock. I struggled to get him to sit down and put on a cold compress. On my hands and knees, as I wiped the trail of his blood from the kitchen floor, I thought, 'Thank God my baby isn't here! Thank God he is not feeling this fear and dread! Thank God he is not smelling this blood! Thank God he is safe somewhere!' Through the years I had a small consolation; I had saved him from harm's way, at the cost of my broken heart.

One breath at a time, one day at a time, I survived. I don't know how I could have done so without my sweet boyfriend always there. With one look, we understood each other.

We built a life together, moved far away; married. We held onto each other; we learned to live and love, always with a deep sorrow in our hearts. We could not bear to talk about our son, each afraid of how hurt the other was by his loss. I silently prayed for our baby and his family. I trusted he was thriving and growing. I searched for him in playgrounds and strollers.

I scanned for news and pictures in the papers. I calculated his age. I read his horoscope. Every child and every age became a reminder of our loss. Is he happy?

When our next sons were born, we watched them with wonder and dreamt again about our baby. Our sorrow was deepened as we learned again, through our children, all we had missed of his life. We learned about all the joys we had lost. Through our other sons, we had a reflection of him and that did offer some comfort.

As we signed the relinquishment papers, the judge emphasized to us that we were *never* to search for him, *never* to contact him, *never* to interrupt his life with his new family. He said he would forget us and it was better for him to be without us, to belong wholly to his new family. We naïvely believed this was the best for him. My adopted friend said she was completely happy with her parents and actually dreaded her original parents ever finding her.

But he did always wonder about us and bravely searched for us. He wrote us a letter. He said he was happy and had had a good life. We were overjoyed, relieved and devastated. We faced again all the sad reasons for his relinquishment. I was plunged into sorrow and bereavement. The delicate scab was ripped off.

He was and is loved by his parents and he loves them too. He grew up strong, capable and mostly happy. But he grew up always wondering about us, always feeling like there was something profoundly, crucially important missing from his life, always missing us, not feeling whole, a little out of synch with his family, never seeing anyone who looked like him, full of questions, forever unanswered. Why could his parents not keep him? What were we like? Why could his grandparents not help or keep him? What kind of person was he, if he came from such people? Did his father abandon his mother, or worse?

When I learned that he painfully suffered the loss of us and had never felt whole, I was devastated. Our sacrifice was meant to keep him whole and safe, yet it didn't.

Our son too must face anew his life story. His parents loved each other and married, without him; he has siblings and wasn't given the chance to grow up with us. His grandparents didn't support his parents or him. No one in his newly found family helped his parents. His parents are good people, but they were not in his life.

He came to see us. For the first time in thirty-five years, we had all of our children together. I was thrilled and devastated, overrun with emotion and pain. We are struggling now to mend our broken hearts, to become a whole family. Progress is slow and uneven.

Many around us do not understand the struggle; they see only a happy reunion. 'Well, it all turned out OK?' They think the story is over – not by a long shot.

My focus now has been to educate people about the pain of adoption. I bear witness whenever I am strong enough to do so. No baby should lose his mother, no parent should have to endure this pain and it certainly is not 'best' for the baby...

~~~

Gina's son was born in the US in 1979

I was seventeen years old in 1978 and living in a small rural Midwestern American town of eight thousand inhabitants, when I became pregnant. The father, Thomas, had been my 'high school sweetheart' and we had been intimate since I was fifteen and he was seventeen. In an attempt to be 'responsible', Thomas and I had secured a prescription for birth control pills – not an easy task at that time or place. One summer day, my mother found them in my dresser drawer and 'all hell broke loose', as they say in that part of the country.

The pills were immediately taken away, the prescribing MD was promptly called and all my dermatology appointments were unilaterally canceled (the latter, a white upper middle-class form of punishment, would have been funny if the consequences of the former had not been so tragic). My already strained relationships with my mother and step-father deteriorated even further.

Yet, we never spoke of the 'incident' again. Although it was 1978 (and, interestingly, the first year in the decline of the number of American adoptions) and the United States had recently experienced the Vietnam War, the resignation of a president over corruption, the rise of 'the counter culture', feminism and civil rights, it was as if this little town was untouched by events it could not directly see or know through its senses. Similar to many rural communities in those days, the church bells still rang out on Sundays, women went about their charity work, the men gathered on Main Street for morning coffee and the local pool hall did not admit women – all remnants from the 1950s in the midst of social, political and economic upheaval and turmoil elsewhere in America and the rest of the world.

I discovered that I was pregnant during the last weeks of my senior year of high school. Given that I had a job as a lifeguard for the summer before I was to go to university in the fall (Thomas was already in university), I decided that I had a window of time to determine if we were going to abort or raise the child – adoption was never an option. After visiting several abortion clinics, we decided this was not our path and that we would raise the child. Neither of us had any religious or other objections to abortion. The option just didn't seem right at the time; even knowing we would need to postpone our education and endure certain hardships, to which neither of us was accustomed.

The day finally arrived when I was forced to reveal my 'secret' to my mother, when she asked what weekend would be best to visit the dorms on campus. Needless to say, the news was not well accepted and all university funds were withdrawn.

A 'meeting' was convened (par for the course for any disturbance in family routines), which consisted of Thomas and his parents, my mother and step-father (my father lived in Florida and, although I loved him very much, he had been estranged for years and would have been of no help in this circumstance) and me. An ultimatum was issued: either get married NOW and live in that town OR leave the house as, "We will not have an unmarried, pregnant daughter parade around town – it's an embarrassment."

I had obviously broken a female moral code of the time and I would be made to pay. Just how dearly a price I would pay was unknown to me at the time. We stated that we would not marry immediately and, as a consequence, I was no longer welcome in the house. I went to live with my extremely supportive grandparents. Both are now deceased, but I still thank them daily for creating a temporary oasis for me, in what was to become a tumultuous storm.

We were young, scared, naïve and without any money (or future funding) except $1,500 I was given from an old child support fund, $1,000 a friend gave us, our savings from our summer jobs and a ¾-ton econo-line Ford van that we purchased from some of our summer savings. The message was quite clear: if you leave, you are on your own. We packed the van and left the Midwest in search of a place more conducive to raising a child and to escape what we perceived as the insanity of our parents' thoughts, beliefs and actions. We headed West and lived in our van for many weeks; sleeping on inflatable pool flotations. We eventually ended up in Mendocino, California where 'like minds of the times' gathered.

As I grew larger, our already short supply of funds shrank even further. Even though Thomas was able to pick up temporary and intermittent painting and carpentry jobs, we were forced to apply for food stamps and welfare for pre-natal medical care. Our parents offered no assistance, except a few dollars from Thomas's father when he begged him to sell some stocks. Oh yes, I was to 'pay' for my 'sins' – and we were.

I spent most of the days of my pregnancy alone, as Thomas was always looking for work or doing an odd job here and there. I mainly read and kept the fire stoked to stay warm, as we could not afford heat nor a heater. In the latter part of my seventh month, the abhorrent realization that we could not afford to take care of ourselves, much less a child, finally surfaced into my consciousness. The only way to give our child a chance in life was 'ADOPTION' – the word itself made me literally ill. I threw up all day when I realized I had no viable choice but to choose this option – an option which had never entered my mind until that day.

ADOPTION SEPARATION

When Thomas returned home that evening, I shared my thoughts, feelings and decision. Not only did he go into a type of denial, but he decided that he would see an attorney to try to reverse my decision and take it upon himself to raise the child. After several days and counseling sessions (paid for by welfare stamps), he reluctantly agreed that adoption was 'best' and we began seeking, via looking through files, 'parents' for our child. We started natural birthing classes (again, paid for by welfare) and painfully tried to brace ourselves for what was about to happen. When we told both our parents about our decision, each offered to raise the child, BUT, did not offer assistance for us to raise the child. I always found and still do find that utterly bizarre!

We chose a name for our son, but his adoptive parents gave him the name Eric. He was born in January, 1979 in California. My labor lasted more than twenty-four hours. The attending MD and two mid-wives conjectured that it was so long because I was unwilling to 'let go' – perceptive on their part! Contrary to earlier practices, I was able to breast feed and Thomas and I were able to hold and bond with our son for several hours. We left the hospital mid-morning the day after his birth and his 'new' parents arrived within two hours of our departure. The 'transfer' was complete. All was signed, all was over. I was numb. I felt like a walking zombie.

Returning to our place without our son after leaving 'with' him less than forty-eight hours prior was surreal. I watched the sunset over the Pacific Ocean the night after returning from the hospital. I watched the beautiful orange being overtaken by darkness, a darkness that would envelope me to varying degrees for years to come. I remember staying in bed for days and then jogging; bed and then jog – like a gerbil's repetitive running in a wheel. I was overwhelmed by outrage, sorrow and disbelief.

Within a year, I (we) had relocated, enrolled in college and had assumed what looked like 'a life'. Yet, I was seeing a therapist, battling anorexia and struggling with depression, attendant with intermittent states of disassociation lasting from one to five minutes. At present, I believe I would have been diagnosed with PTSD. However, in those days, that diagnosis was not recognized in such circumstances. There was a laissez-faire attitude of 'just get on with your life' or 'you just committed the most selfish or selfless (according to whoever was talking) act of your life'.

I managed to finish university and go on to attain two Master degrees and a Ph.D.. Although I naturally excelled in academia, my drive came from a place much deeper within – 'a pact with the devil', as I have always termed it. The pact: if I was going to relinquish my son so that he would have a shot at a good education, which I felt I could not provide at the time, then I had to accomplish those degrees myself – almost an act of atonement. Logical? NO. Common guilt-driven pact/behavior? YES.

Thomas and I eventually married and then divorced a few years later. We both re-married (other people), but neither of us have children, as we both felt that it would be a betrayal to Eric (also a common feeling among birth parents). Both our spouses have been extremely supportive regarding our past experiences and the despair that would set in around his birthday and other holidays. I was in and out of therapy for several years, but none of it really made a difference in my life, as no one I saw understood the severe emotional and psychological impact of adoption.

Thankfully, times have changed and there are now wonderful therapists who specialize specifically in adoption issues. During all those years of graduate school, degrees, my own private practice and professorships, I was always uncomfortable around children and I NEVER talked about my experiences with anyone, except a very select few. It was my guilty, shameful secret which unconsciously colored my entire life. Even to this day, my step-father has never mentioned the adoption.

Four and a half years ago, I received an ecstatic and elated call from a friend who had also relinquished her son in California under similar circumstances. After years of searching, her son had finally found her. I quickly learned from her that all the laws regarding adoption had changed and that all I had left for Eric to review when he was eighteen years old was no longer in existence. I would have to go through all the paper work again. Up until that time, I had 'assumed' that he had the information necessary to contact me and that he had 'chosen' not to pursue a reunion, or couldn't because of some unknown reason, or he was dead – the most dreadful thought possible. I, therefore, didn't search, as I didn't want to 'invade his privacy' – another misperception held by many birth parents.

In fact, he did file search paperwork when he was twenty-one years old with the help of his adoptive father. Within hours of knowing about the new laws, I filed the necessary papers and started searching for him. Something transformed in my heart and NOTHING was going to stop me from finding him. Within three weeks he had received my 'phone number and address. Within four weeks, he e-mailed and we spoke on the 'phone. Within eight weeks, my husband and I flew my twenty-seven year old son to our home in Hawaii for our reunion.

There are simply no words to describe seeing and hugging your child, now a young man, for the first time since saying goodbye to him as a day-old baby. There are simply no words to describe the bursting forth of love, energy, aliveness, amazement and, yes, shock as well. It was the single most important and greatest moment of my life.

Eric and I eventually ended up talking for hours and comparing fingers, toes and ears during his first trip, of many, to the islands. He told me as much as possible, at the time, about his childhood, growing up and his relationship to his adoptive parents. His adoptive mother had even sent a photo album with him, so that I could view the different stages of his life. Both of his adoptive parents have been supportive of close contact between Eric and myself, as well as themselves. I met his adoptive mother during a trip to visit Eric and his partner and she and I exchanged gifts and had a wonderful lunch together.

Now we exchange Christmas cards and e-mails. Although Eric and I have discovered many similarities in preferences about many matters, probably the most eerie discoveries were, that we graduated from the same undergraduate institution, that my first professor there was his last, that he had lived on Maui for several years while I lived on Oahu and that he grew up and now lives three hours from where his birth father, Thomas, now resides.

After his first trip to Oahu, he met Thomas for the first time about a week later. Because of their proximity and bond, they pal around together quite frequently.

It has been four years since our 'reunion' and although the 'honeymoon stage' is over, our connection has strengthened and grown stronger – albeit, not without some bumps along the way! One of the main hurdles to surpass during the first year was his sense of obligation to assuage the pain Thomas and I had experienced. This is not uncommon for an adoptee.

After these and some other issues were sorted through and some necessary distancing for a short period of time, all now feels very natural and integrated – like the family it IS, not the family that it could have been, but IS.

In all my years in academia and even during my years in practice as a psychotherapist, I had not picked up nor read one book on adoption. I did not speak on the topic and, if it arose, I switched the topic. Since the reunion with Eric, I have read everything I can get my hands on, speak freely about the topic and my experiences with many different types of people, write on the topic and have joined a triad group which includes all members of the adoption circle, including a therapist.

The forbidden, guilt-producing, crippling, immobilizing, shame-inducing, 'secret' is gone. This is not to say that I still do not struggle, because at times I do, especially in my relationship with my mother.

However, my struggles are not with my own closeted demons. They are openly human struggles which are part of the healing process.

I urge everyone, in any part of the triad, or who is in any kind of relation with those affected by adoption, to educate themselves (ignorance is NOT bliss) and to discuss their experiences.

A safe environment in which to speak is very important at the beginning. Also to write about their situation(s) – journaling is a wonderful way to begin the healing process.

The healing journey is long and not easy, by any means; pre, post, or no reunion at all. It takes courage. But, when you feel your heart break open with a 'lightness' – even if for brief moments – rather than hollow with empty yet onerous space in your soul, you'll know. You'll know all the hard work the journey requires is worth it!

~~~~

Carlynne's daughter was born in the US in 1980

In 1979 I was an art major in college. At the age of nineteen I was still a virgin and a good Catholic girl. There was no talk about birth control when I was growing up – of course not – I was expected to remain a virgin until the day I married. When I finally decided to 'lose it' I used my limited knowledge about natural family planning or the rhythm method, so the result...the first time I slept with J, I got pregnant. Obviously my knowledge was lacking.

Terror was the only word I can use to describe what I felt. By the time I found out I was pregnant, J had graduated from school and moved on and I was back home living with my family. Mom guessed my condition before I could tell her. When I admitted my condition, harsh things were said and it was made clear that I could not bring my baby back home. I couldn't find J since he was states away and the school wouldn't give me any forwarding contact information.

At this point I was so scared and naïve that I just did what I was told. My home was my only place of security. I didn't have extended family close by; they lived on the other side of the country – all the easier to hide my condition. No one was to know that I was pregnant. I couldn't tell a soul. I don't know if they were trying to protect me from the scandal or just protecting themselves from the shame. I had shamed the family; I was a disgrace. Once I began to show and I was going to have to wear maternity clothes, I was not supposed to leave the house. I couldn't attend church. I basically became a prisoner in my own home.

It was decided that the best thing to do was to leave town and give my child up for adoption through Catholic Social Services (CSS). My parents drove me several hours from home to live with an older woman who took in unwed, pregnant girls. This was all arranged through CSS.

They left me there with my suitcase in hand, looking at this stranger. M was a nice woman. We sat night after night, her drinking her highball, me drinking my chocolate milk. I dusted and vacuumed, occasionally cooked. I went on her Meals on Wheels runs with her. It was a quiet time, at least on the surface. I didn't talk much; couldn't talk much. It was like I went into robot mode – auto-pilot. I wrote letters home (that I have no memory of writing and they were even in a handwriting that didn't look familiar) that regurgitated everything I was being told – this is the best thing for the baby, a child needs both parents, it's an unselfish thing to do etc, etc…

Recently, for the first time in thirty years I was able to get a copy of the paperwork that I signed relating to the adoption. One piece of paper astounded me. Again I have no memory of signing it, but it was a consent to release custody and control of the child to CSS. It was dated three full months before my daughter was born! They actually got me to sign a custody release when I was six months' pregnant. I don't know how those people slept at night. Maybe they really believed they were doing the right thing by pushing me to do it. I hope they know better now.

When I went into labor M took me to the hospital, sat with me for a short time and left. I labored alone and delivered my baby to a stranger. I had never met the doctor before delivery. The nurses took her, wrapped her in a blanket and whisked her away. I was not allowed to see her or hold her. They wouldn't even tell me if it was a boy or girl. I never knew her weight, length or if she was OK. I heard her cry shortly after she was born and I saw one little arm peeking out of the blanket as they turned and walked away. Not a word was said to me. I was like a thing, a manufacturer of goods.

I tore badly during delivery and the doctor had to do quite a bit of sewing. There was no anesthesia used for that. As I cried and yelled, the doctor yelled back at me to be quiet and move down on the table.

I was taken to my room, which was right next to the nursery. I could hear the babies crying. It was torture. I tried to keep my door closed, but every time I closed it the nurses would come along and open it again. On the door to my room was a piece of red construction paper with BFA – baby for adoption – in big black letters. Another BFA sign was posted above the headboard of my bed. This was to alert the staff to be sure they didn't bring my baby to me or tell me anything about her.

One day as I was walking down the hall, one of the nurses had a clipboard and was getting consent forms signed for circumcision on the boys. I didn't know what she was doing. She asked my name and when I told her she said, "Oh, you don't have to worry about this, you had a girl." That's how I found out the sex of my child.

Then and now

Four days after my daughter's birth I was taken to the CSS office and given papers to sign. During my five-month stay at the home I was never given any counseling, other than being told that this was the best thing to do for my child. That's not counseling. I wasn't given any options, wasn't offered any information on what help was available if I wanted to keep my child. It was just a foregone conclusion that this was going to happen.

In the office there was no legal representation, no one there but the woman who handed me the papers to sign. I was sobbing so hard I couldn't see anything. All I remember is putting my name on the line and the woman handing me a box of tissues. She didn't say anything. There were no words of comfort. I was not given a copy of anything I signed. Not long after that my family came to pick me up. I left M and we drove home in silence. Not a word was said; I was to pretend that nothing had happened. As far as friends and extended family were concerned I had been away at a job in an advertising agency and was now home to stay.

The year following my daughter's birth was the closest I'd ever come to contemplating suicide. I don't think anyone can really understand what a mother of adoption loss goes through unless she's been there too. I used to liken it to losing a child to death, but that's not right. It's more like a secret kidnapping. When a child dies a mother mourns her loss, she has comfort and friends and family acknowledge the grief.

In the case of adoption the grief goes on forever, even after reunion. You're expected to just get on with your life, get over it, have more children and you'll forget. These are the lies we're told. People look at us as if we're crazy, wondering why we just don't leave the past in the past and this is only if we feel like we can tell some people about our loss. Most people have no idea what we live with.

When my daughter turned eighteen I made a birthday cake for her and my other two children and I sang *Happy Birthday*

215

to her. That was the beginning of my search for her. I had told my husband and children about her. My friends also knew and by this time my extended family knew. No one wanted to disown me; some of them wished I had told them back then. No one was going to make me keep this secret ever again. I spent four years searching and finally, when she was twenty-two, we made contact.

I'll never forget the day I got the call that she wanted to know me. The joy was unbelievable. Nothing can compare to the relief of finding your own child. I felt like I had just been released from a twenty-two year prison sentence.

She is now part of my family. We've been reunited for eight years and it's been wonderful. I'm truly thankful to have her back in my life but those twenty-two years can never be returned to either one of us. She lost not only her mother but also her entire family. I was told both adoptive parents would raise her; she would have a stable two-parent home.

Adoptive families are no different from the rest of the population. Their divorce rate is no less. My daughter was taken from me and still a single mother raised her.

The only difference between me and the woman who adopted my daughter is that I had the nerve to be pregnant and unmarried.

My daughter was born in 1980 in the United States. Some people find that hard to believe. Yes, women and girls were still treated this way in the '80s. It's going on now.

This multi-billion dollar industry is still working its magic and making people believe that taking babies away from their mothers is a good and noble thing. It was coercive then and it's coercive now. **It's not noble; it's a tragedy.**

Adoption in the 21st Century

ADOPTION SEPARATION

Then and now

Adoption separation, now

The first section of this book, **Adoption separation, then**, contains the words and thoughts of others about adoption in the twentieth century. This second section contains my words and thoughts about several aspects of adoption in the twenty-first century.

There have been enormous social changes since the middle of the twentieth century. The ideal of the traditional, nuclear family is less dominant than it was. Many children do not live with both of their parents in the same home and it is not uncommon for siblings to have different fathers and different surnames. The stigma attached to illegitimacy has all but disappeared and we are more tolerant of different family structures.

The influence of religion has reduced noticeably in the major English-speaking countries and there is much less shame and guilt attached to sexual behaviour. Social activism has increased awareness of the long term grief and loss associated with adoption separation and has changed attitudes to parenting.

Some of those who want children and are unwilling or unable to produce them by natural means are now using scientific means, such as donor conception and surrogacy to 'create a family'. Medical science has to some extent replaced religion as a vehicle for providing children. Adults who were created by these methods are now experiencing feelings of genealogical displacement, similar to those experienced by adults who were adopted as children.

ADOPTION SEPARATION

*The parents who have contributed their stories for this book have described how they were advised to put their experiences of birth and adoption behind them and 'get on with their lives'. Clearly, this was an unrealistic and unhealthy expectation. It is obvious that these parents cared about their lost children and continued to experience feelings of grief around the separation, often for many years. In **Picking up the pieces**, I explain how, in most locations, there is now an official recognition of the losses created by adoption separation and attempts are being made by governments to help those affected to manage those losses.*

*In spite of the knowledge we now have about the long term impact of adoption separation, there are still children being born and adopted in the countries represented here. However, each country manages adoptions in its own way. More than half of the adoptions described in this book occurred in Australia and the United States. In **Different approaches**, I compare the way adoptions are managed in the twenty-first century in these two countries.*

*Tragically, there are locations in the world where women are still being shamed and blamed for becoming pregnant and are labelled immoral or irresponsible. They are being punished by having their children taken from them. Many people are striving to highlight the social inequities of present day adoptions. However, there are societies which have very different attitudes to parenting than our traditional western approach. In the chapter entitled, **In the country of daughters**, I describe one such society, in which not only are all babies born given an equally warm welcome into the world, but women are traditionally expected to have many sexual partners.*

Then and now

In the countries represented in this book, the number of children born to unmarried parents has increased considerably in recent years. At the same time, the number of children born in those countries, who are being adopted, has decreased. In the twentieth century, adoption was widely considered to be in the best interests of many children, especially those whose parents were not married. In the twenty-first century, we understand that loving care, combined with genealogical continuity, are actually in the best interests of children. This is another reason for the reduction in the number of adoptions in Australia.

The number of children being adopted within the countries represented in this book began to reduce around the middle of the 1970s. Subsequently, those wishing to adopt began to identify other countries with which adoption arrangements could be developed. In **The intercountry stolen generation**, I have highlighted some of the outcomes of these arrangements.

Finally, in 2010, Western Australia became the first government in the world to apologise officially to those whose lives had been adversely affected by past adoption policies and practices. In **The Times They Are A-Changin'**, I explain how and why that happened and what it might mean for the future.

I hope that my readers will gain a deeper understanding of the global impact of adoption, in both the past and the present centuries and that this understanding can be used to ensure that, in the near future, adoption, in every country in the world, will cease to be used to separate children from their mothers, fathers, families and heritage and will be replaced by more child-centred alternatives.

ADOPTION SEPARATION

Picking up the pieces

Over the years, those who have experienced adoption separation have worked together and set up support organisations to share their healing. They have also lobbied their governments to pass legislation to allow information to be shared once the child who was adopted becomes an adult and to fund services to assist with the recovery process. Organisations and individuals have worked hard for many years, to try to increase awareness of the long term outcomes of adoption separation and of the need for governments to take responsibility for repairing the emotional damage caused by past adoption policies and practices.

In South Australia, there is a *Post Adoption Support Service*, which is fully funded by the state government. They provide counselling, support groups and assistance and support with search and reunion to anyone who has experienced an adoption separation, as well as training in post-adoption issues for professionals. There is also the *Adoption and Family Information Service*, which is the government body responsible for providing legal documents relating to adoption, such as adoption records and the necessary paperwork needed to access further information. Most other states and territories in Australia have similar services. In the other countries represented here, there are also services which are provided by both government and non-government agencies, although these are not always accompanied by specialised counselling services.

This is a summary of the information I have been able to gather. Adoption legislation is frequently changing and so it is impossible to guarantee that this information is current and accurate.

ADOPTION SEPARATION

In Australia

The South Australian government was the first in the world to pass legislation lifting the restrictions which prevented mothers who had lost children to adoption from knowing the new identity of their child, once the adopted child had reached adulthood.

Mothers who have lost children to adoption in South Australia have had a legal right, once their children become adults (currently at the age of eighteen) to receive a copy of their child's amended birth certificate (ie the one which is issued after the adoption takes place and supersedes the original birth certificate), since the passing of the *Adoption Act 1988*. This allows the mother to know the new name given to the child after the adoption, the names of the adoptive parents and their address at the time of the adoption. Most other states and territories in Australia have since passed similar legislation.

Adults who were adopted as children in South Australia have a similar legal right, when they are adults, to receive a copy of their original birth certificate. This will provide the name they were given at birth, as well as the name and address of their mother at the time of their birth. Other information from the adoption file is often also available.

For adoptions which took place prior to the passing of this act, either party ie the adult who was adopted as a child or the original mother, can lodge a veto, which prevents this information being released to the other. For adoptions which have taken place since the *Adoption Act 1988* was passed, however, it is not possible for either party to be prevented from receiving this information.

The children of an adult who was adopted as a child and any other children born to a mother who lost a child to adoption have a legal right to access identifying information, either with the permission of the party involved in the adoption separation or after their death.

Then and now

In Canada

In Canada, in recent years, most territories and provinces have passed legislation which allows mothers access to identifying information about the children they lost to adoption, once those children are adults. This legislation also ensures that adults who were adopted as children, when they reach adulthood, can access identifying information about their original mothers. In some areas, however, this only applies to more recent adoptions.

In each area where such legislation exists, the release of information can be prevented by the lodgement of a veto, by one of the parties involved. In Alberta, the adoptive parents can lodge a veto, which prevents their adult adopted children from obtaining information about their origins, if the adoptive parents have chosen not to tell them that they are adopted. In some areas, other family members are also eligible to receive identifying information. It is not possible, however, for original mothers to obtain identifying information about adoptive parents.

In some locations, it is not possible to access identifying information, but there are various types of contact registers. Wherever they exist, these have some significant limitations. For example, adoptive parents may not have disclosed to children that they have been adopted, or death could occur before people are eligible to add their names to a register. Also, such registers are not widely publicised and many people are unaware that they exist.

In England

In England, adults who were adopted as children have been able to access their original birth certificates, when they reach adulthood, since 1975. However, mothers who have lost children to adoption in England have no right to be advised of the new identity given to their children after the adoption took place.

ADOPTION SEPARATION

There is an adoption contact register and mothers may approach an adoption service and ask them to search for and contact the adult child who was adopted. If an approach to an adult adopted child is requested, the agency controls how, when and, ultimately, if this takes place. It is not surprising that people use private investigators and internet sites as a way of circumventing this process and taking control.

Adults who were adopted as children can lodge a veto, which prevents any intermediary service from making contact with them. Mothers, however, are unable to lodge vetoes. Children of either the mother or the adopted adult have no right to receive identifying information.

In Ireland

In Ireland, neither adults who were adopted as children, nor mothers who have lost children to adoption have any legal right to access any identifying information which would allow them to trace and/or contact each other. They may, however, approach adoption services and request that they trace family members from whom they have been separated by adoption.

There is also an official contact preference register. Anyone who has experienced adoption separation can add their contact details to the register and indicate whether or not they would like to be contacted. If a match is made, contact can be made through an agency, which, of course, controls the contact process.

In New Zealand

Adults who were adopted as children in New Zealand have a legal right to obtain their original birth certificate, which contains information about their original mother at the time of the adoption, when they are aged twenty.

Their original mother can prevent them from receiving any information which would identify her, if the adoption took place before 1986.

A mother who has lost a child to adoption in New Zealand has no legal right to receive information which would identify that adult child, unless the child is already dead when the mother applies. The mother may request that a social worker try to locate and contact an adult child, who is still living, to ascertain whether or not the child is willing for identifying information to be released to the mother.

In Scotland

In Scotland, adults who were adopted as children have had a legal right to obtain their original birth certificates, which give identifying information about their original mothers, since the passing of the *Adoption Act 1930*.

However, as in England, mothers who have lost children to adoption in Scotland have no right to know the new identity given to their children after the adoption took place. Children of either the mother or the adopted adult have no right to receive identifying information.

There are some services which can assist with search and reunion, but they maintain the right to control and manage the process and to refuse to assist. There is also a contact register.

In the United States

Nowhere in the United States do mothers who have lost children to adoption have a legal right to obtain the replacement birth certificate issued to their child, once that child becomes an adult.

In the state of Alaska, a mother who has lost a child to adoption may request the new name given to the child after adoption, when that child is aged eighteen. The name will only be released to the mother, however, if the adult child has given written permission. Adults who were adopted as children in Alaska may have access to their original birth certificates, when they are aged eighteen. Either party to the adoption can lodge updated contact details with the relevant department at any time and these will also be provided to anyone who qualifies for identifying information.

In approximately forty states, there exists a 'mutual consent registry', which is a form of contact register. Although these vary slightly from state to state, generally, where one exists, identifying information can be released, by consent, when the adopted child is an adult. This means that identifying information will be released by an agency, if the party in question has given written consent for this to happen, providing that the agency does not deem this to be inappropriate.

In some states, counselling is compulsory before adoption information is released. In most of these states, other children born to the mother may also access identifying information, on a 'mutual consent' basis.

Some states will release information, under certain circumstances, to a 'confidential intermediary'. In some states, information will not be released if the other party is deceased.

I believe that there are only nine states in which adults who were adopted as children have a legal right to access their original birth certificates. In some states the original birth certificate can be accessed only via a court order and in some states it cannot be accessed at all.

Access to information can be restricted in other ways. In Nebraska, adoptive parents can sign a document which prevents the adopted child from being able to access their original birth certificate until after the death of the adoptive parents.

In New Jersey and the District of Columbia (DC), all adoption information is 'sealed' and can only be opened by a court order.

Then and now

Summary

It is clear that, in many locations, there is a recognition that accessing information can assist in the recovery and healing process, for those separated from family members by adoption. Unfortunately, in some places, there are restrictions around the release and use of such information. Many of those affected find these restrictions demeaning and insulting.

There are few jurisdictions in the world where mothers are allowed by law to obtain information which would allow them to trace and contact their adult adopted children, at a time and in a manner which they believe to be appropriate. Instead, the process is too often controlled for them by government employees or staff of adoption services, who may not be appropriately trained in adoption loss and reunion and who may allow personal bias to influence their decision-making.

Sadly, this system disempowers and punishes mothers, quite unjustifiably, by preventing them from conducting their reunions with their adult children in their own way and according to their understanding of the issues. Paradoxically, many of them were considered to be responsible enough, when they were much younger, to make a major life-altering decision for themselves and their children, but are then deemed incompetent in later life to be trusted to handle information about those now adult children with discretion and consideration. This attitude perpetuates the blaming and shaming of original mothers of adopted children.

It is also extremely difficult to locate helpful professionals who have an understanding of adoption loss and recovery issues, which is why self-help books on these topics are so popular.

It is to be hoped that all governments will soon recognise their responsibilities to provide adequate funding for appropriate counselling services for those whose lives have been affected by adoption separation and will pass legislation which allows them to make informed, autonomous choices around contact and reunion.

Different approaches

The narratives in this book start with Australia and end with the United States and I received more contributions from those locations than any other. I am often asked about current adoption policy and practice in these two countries and how they differ.

I recognise that domestic adoption policy is, in both places, subject to state rather than federal legislation and so there are variations in policy and practice from state to state. My comments are, therefore, of a general nature only, as I appreciate that there are many local variations.

I am most familiar with policy and practice in my home state of South Australia, but I am aware that most other states and territories in Australia operate in similar ways. Adoption policy and practice in South Australia are based on the *Adoption Act 1988* and have been in effect since that act was passed in 1989. Since 1989, it has been possible to appraise and monitor the outcomes of this legislation and the act was officially reviewed in 1994.

Private adoptions are illegal in all states and territories in Australia and all domestic adoptions are arranged by State Government departments. There are no commercially-based adoption agencies which are licensed to manage these adoptions.

In contrast, in the United States, private adoption agencies are licensed to arrange domestic adoptions. Because adoption has been allowed to acquire a commercial status in the United States, there are financial advantages for agencies in arranging as many adoptions as possible. Adoption agencies in the United States, therefore, have an incentive to attract customers, just as any other business does.

Many people have expressed to me that they find the fact that money and children change hands in the same transactions to be at the very least distasteful, if not, in fact, immoral. Sometimes prospective adoptive parents are encouraged to offer financial incentives to expectant mothers to try to persuade them to agree to an adoption.

Expectant mothers in Australia, regardless of their circumstances, are generally encouraged and supported to prepare for raising their children. After the birth, a Parenting Payment is available from the Federal Government to anyone, regardless of their gender or marital status, who is a permanent resident of Australia and who has custody of a child. This payment, which is means-tested, is a recognition by the Australian government that children are the basis of a country's future. The government, therefore, makes financial support available to parents to assist them to provide for their children. As far as I am aware, there is no corresponding payment available at a Federal Government level in the United States, although I have been advised that there may be tax benefits for parents who are in paid employment.

While there is still a degree of disapproval in some quarters towards single parenthood, there is a much greater level of acceptance in Australia than there was in the past. For this and other reasons, there has been a dramatic decrease in the number of adoptions in Australia over the last forty years. In 2010, in the state of South Australia (which has a population of more than two million people), for example, only one Australian-born child was adopted.

The term 'birthmother' (or 'birth mother') is currently out of favour with many of the support groups in Australia and certainly would never be used, as I have heard it used in the United States, to describe an expectant mother. I have even heard the term 'birthmother-to-be' used to describe a pregnant woman. This sinister use of the term 'birthmother', before the birth has even taken place, implies that the separation of mother and child is a foregone conclusion. Expectant mothers in Australia, on the other hand, are generally encouraged to concentrate on their approaching motherhood throughout their pregnancies and no decisions regarding their child's future are expected to be made until after the birth has occurred.

I have been advised that, in the United States, fathers who are not married to the mothers of their children have a difficult time being heard. In South Australia, an unmarried mother who is considering adoption will always be asked to name the child's father and attempts will be made to include him in the decision-making process. If the father is named on the birth certificate or if a man is recognised by the court as being the father of a child, then his consent is necessary before that child can be adopted. The father will be allowed time to establish paternity. If the father wishes to raise the child, he has the right to do so. If the mother and father do not agree with regard to the child's future, the matter may be decided by the Family Court. This would happen before any consent to adoption had been completed.

In South Australia, under the *Adoption Act 1988*, consent to adoption cannot be given until the child is at least fourteen days old. Counselling after the birth is compulsory and must be completed at least three days prior to consent being given. The mother of the child must also be given information, in writing, regarding the consequences of the adoption, prior to any taking of consent. After the consent has been signed there is a period of twenty-five days during which the consent may be revoked. This period can be extended by up to fourteen days, but it cannot be shortened.

In practice, the consent to adoption is sometimes not finalised until several months after the birth. While this may not be an ideal situation, it is felt to be of prime importance that children have every opportunity to be raised within their families of origin. This will prevent the long term complexities in the lives of those children and their parents, which would occur if an adoption took place. During this period the child may remain with the mother and/or father. Situations in which children are adopted without the consent of their parents are very rare. I have heard of cases in the United States, tragically, in which adoption consents have been signed even before the birth, or very soon after the birth. I have also heard of cases where attempts to revoke the consent the day after it had been signed have failed.

In Australia there is never any contact of any kind between expectant mothers and prospective adopters. I know that there are many who agree with me that such contacts could be not only intrusive and disempowering to the expectant mother, but also exploitative. They may even serve to encourage an inappropriate sense of 'ownership' in the prospective adopters, which, I believe, shows a lack of respect for and understanding of the sanctity of the mother/child bond.

In South Australia, only after the consent to adoption has been signed and after the twenty-five day revocation period has expired will the government department involved select adopters for the child. After this decision has been made, a meeting may take place between the prospective adopters who have been selected and the mother, if the mother requests such a meeting. Prospective adopters will not have any contact at all with the child until after the revocation period has expired and they have been notified that they have been selected to adopt.

I find it hard to understand how anyone can support the practice of having prospective adopters meet with expectant mothers and try to induce them to consent to the adoption of the child they are carrying. I believe that prospective adopters are sometimes even allowed to be present at the hospital while the birth is taking place. I was appalled to hear that this happens in the United States. I find such behaviour totally inappropriate and unethical. It concerns me greatly that prospective adopters who behave in this way are not thereby considered as unsuitable to adopt.

233

ADOPTION SEPARATION

In South Australia, if the adopters are willing, they can have their names added to the child's original birth certificate instead of having a new one issued. This means that, after the adoption, the names of both the original parents and the adoptive parents appear on the same document, which is the child's legal birth certificate. The mother of the child has access to the original birth certificate from the time that the birth is registered. The father also has access if his name appears on the birth certificate.

Regardless of the type of birth certificate issued, adults who were adopted as children in South Australia have a legal right to obtain their original birth certificates and other documentation pertaining to their adoption, when they are eighteen years old. The original birth certificate has details of their parents, including their names and addresses at the time of the adoption. They may have access prior to the age of eighteen with the consent of both their adoptive parents and their original parents.

The original mother of the adopted child also has a legal right to obtain the replacement birth certificate when the adopted child becomes an adult, at the age of eighteen years. This document has details of the child's adopted name, the names of the adoptive parents and their address at the time of the adoption.

These documents are also available to any other children of the original mother, either if the mother gives permission or after her death and to the children of an adopted adult, if the adopted adult gives permission or after their death. Fathers also have the right to access information about their children under certain circumstances. The legislation which allows this access has been in effect in South Australia since 1989. It is a fair and just piece of legislation, which supports healing.

There are now some states in the United States where adults who were adopted as children are allowed to obtain their original birth certificates, but there are no states in which parents have a legal right to access the replacement birth certificates once their children are adults. I look forward to the time when equal access to adoption information, such as exists in South Australia, will be accepted as a basic human right everywhere in the United States. This is an on-going issue of social justice.

I was very shocked to learn that, in the United States, parents who are married and already have children are being persuaded to relinquish newly-born infants. The subsequent separation of such a child from a previously intact family is causing enormous losses, for the child, for the parents, for the other children in the family, for the grandparents as well as many other members of the extended family. This does not, to my knowledge, happen anywhere in Australia.

Apparently, having children while on a low income is now perceived as such a crime in some parts of the United States, that this dreadful punishment has been devised. If poverty is considered to be a disadvantage to such children, then government initiatives which address the issue of poverty would be more useful to them, than replacing the complications created in their lives by poverty with the complications created by adoption.

While there are many in the United States who are working hard in family preservation programmes to prevent separations of mothers and babies, I am saddened by the fact that there are still those who believe that adoption is an appropriate outcome for older children for whom it is considered to be unsafe to live with their families. Adoption is rarely considered to be an appropriate outcome for such children in Australia.

I have heard it said in the United States that adoption can provide such children with a sense of security. In fact, in my opinion, the opposite is the case. Children such as these know who they are and to whom they are related. These realities do not change, no matter where the child is living. To deny that identity and those connections by issuing the child with a false birth certificate has, in fact, the potential to create an enormous sense of insecurity. If their identity and their family connections are so dispensable, then how can a child in this situation develop any sense of reality and permanence? We all know that being part of an adoptive family does not provide protection against abuse, death or divorce. Adoption, in fact, does not guarantee permanence of any kind and is actually a way of creating legal relationships where none existed previously, rather than honouring those relationships which already exist.

In Australia, children for whom it is considered to be unsafe to live with their families of origin can be provided with a different family environment, under a permanent guardianship order. This is an arrangement which accepts and honours the reality of the child's identity and their existing relationships. This, I believe, can allow them to heal and recover without involving them in the pretence and denial associated with adoption.

Under a permanent guardianship order, the guardians have all the rights and responsibilities of parents, but the children retain their original identities and their original birth certificates. They also maintain all their legal relationships within their families of origin. This means that there is no need for the creation of a new, false identity and no need for the children to sever relationships with all members of their original families such as siblings, cousins and grandparents. There are significant advantages to children who are considered to be unsafe living in their families of origin to be cared for in this way. It is truly a child-centred option and suggests to me that Australians respect the importance of heritage and genealogical continuity and the intrinsic value of identity and family membership.

It is not considered to be appropriate in Australia to try to solve the problems of poverty and abuse in families, by removing children and arranging for them to be adopted. The number of domestic adoptions in South Australia has reduced from almost one thousand per year in 1970 to one per year in 2010.

Adoption is not a commercial transaction in Australia and it is gradually being replaced by other, more honest and child-centred means of providing homes for children in need.

In the country of daughters

It is clear from the narratives contained in this book that most of the parents who lost their children to adoption in the twentieth century had violated a strict social code and, because of this, found themselves unsupported and vulnerable. It was very easy, therefore, for that vulnerability to be exploited. Had their children been born in a different place, or in a different time, the outcome might have been quite different.

After seeing a fascinating documentary on television, in 2003, about the Moso people and their culture, I wanted to learn more. I found a book called *Leaving Mother Lake – A Girlhood at the Edge of the World*. The book is written as a memoir by Yang Erche Namu, a young woman who was born and raised in a Moso village in southern China, near the Tibetan border. Namu wrote the book when she was twenty-seven years old and living in San Francisco. Namu was assisted to write the book by Christine Mathieu, who is a lecturer in anthropology at St Mary's College in California. Christine completed her doctoral studies in anthropology among the Moso people. Namu told Christine her story and together they created this book.

The Chinese call the isolated area where the Moso people live 'The Country of Daughters'. The Moso people live a simple, agricultural life and their family structure is matriarchal. There is a written history of this matriarchal society which goes back to the sixth century, although it may well have been in existence for much longer. The Moso people still practise their ancient traditions today, in spite of the fact that their ways may seem unusual to the rest of the world.

Mothers are the head of the family unit among the Moso people. Adult males and females remain in the family home with their mothers. Children are raised with their mothers in an extended family situation, which includes their aunts and uncles, cousins and, of course, their grandmother. Children take their names from their mothers and they inherit from their mothers.

The Moso are a peaceful, polite people. There is no marriage among the Moso people and their language has no word for 'father', as we define it. In their community there are no expressions of sexual jealousy and no murders.

The Moso believe that women carry the seeds of their children within them from the time of their birth and that, as stated by one Moso grandmother in the television documentary, "It doesn't matter who waters the seed."

When Moso girls reach puberty, the whole village celebrates their Skirt Ceremony. This is a joyful occasion, involving eating, drinking and the giving of gifts. The Skirt Ceremony signifies to the community that the young woman is now ready to take lovers. Once a daughter has become a woman in this way, she is given her own room in the family home, in which she shares time with her lovers, by firelight.

The Moso are a modest people and sexual behaviour is expected to be conducted in private. A potential lover knocks on the window of the room belonging to a young woman who appeals to him, late in the evening, after the family has retired. If the young woman is willing, she opens her door to him. They spend the night together and he leaves in the morning, before the family rises. In this way love affairs are undertaken in a manner that does not interfere with the family, which is the foundation of the Moso community.

Moso women usually have many lovers and may have many children. Their families are proud of this behaviour, as it is in accordance with Moso tradition and so they are fulfilling the expectations with which they have been raised.

Then and now

In contrast to most Western societies, there is no shame or guilt attached to such sexual conduct. In fact, the behaviour which gains approval in Moso culture, has traditionally produced disapproval in most other cultures.

The only relationships which are forbidden among the Moso, as they are in most cultures, are relationships between siblings. The Moso have no concept of marriage or illegitimacy. Every baby born is welcomed, cherished and celebrated with pride, as a joyful addition to the family.

Learning about the Moso people has reinforced for me the fact that the practice of adoption is too often a social construction, linked to the guilt and shame which is attached to certain sexual behaviour in some societies. The stigma attached to ex-nuptial births, which led to so many adoptions in the second half of the twentieth century, existed in particular places in the world and at a particular time in history.

While Moso traditions have remained the same for hundreds of years, attitudes in our society have altered significantly in recent decades. If those who lost children through adoption had become mothers in another geographical location or at a time when our society's expectations were less rigid, the outcome for them and for their children might have been radically different.

Their children could have been welcomed and accepted and, instead of being separated from them, they could have been honoured and celebrated as their proud mothers.

ADOPTION SEPARATION

The intercountry stolen generation

Children are dependent and vulnerable and so governments have a responsibility to put in place policies which will protect them from harm. In recent years, Australia has been revisiting past policies and practices around the care of vulnerable and unprotected children. The Australian experience of family separation in the twentieth century can teach the world a great deal.

Under child migration schemes, children who had been in care in Britain, after the Second World War, were brought out to Australia to live. Some of those children were placed with families and some were placed in institutions. This occurred because those children had been separated from their parents and were therefore vulnerable and unprotected. These schemes ended in the early 1970s.

Australian Aboriginal children were removed from their families, especially in the earlier part of the twentieth century. Some were raised in institutions and some in non-Aboriginal foster homes. Those children were vulnerable because they were Aboriginal. This practice continued until approximately 1970, creating what became known as the Stolen Generations.

Children were removed from their families because of child protection issues and cared for in institutions. This occurred because they were considered to be at risk if they remained with their parents. Many of those children were mistreated and unnecessarily separated from family members and are now known as the Forgotten Australians. This practice also ceased towards the end of the twentieth century.

Then and now

We have since created more child-centred options for children at risk and more support for families experiencing difficulties.

The outcome of all of these major family separation experiences has been long term grief and loss. These losses have been acknowledged by Federal Government apologies in the twenty-first century to the British Child Migrants, the Forgotten Australians and to the Stolen Generations. Apologies have been considered to be appropriate, because these practices were considered not to have been in the best interests of the children and families involved. The fact that government apologies have been made is an indication that the values which underpinned the actions of those responsible for these family separations, which occurred in the last century, are not considered to be acceptable today.

Loss and grief are both personal and communal. For each of the children involved in these family separations, many others are also affected. The effects of separation are felt at many levels. These events have had a significant impact on Australia as a nation. The outcomes of these past policies have been documented and made public, leading to the Federal Government apologies, which we have witnessed and welcomed.

Many thousands of babies were removed from their unsupported, unmarried mothers in Australia during the twentieth century, especially between 1965 and 1975. The vast majority of those children were adopted. Unsupported, unmarried mothers were considered to be incompetent and were rendered powerless owing to their lack of information, community support and resources. Their punishment was to have their children removed from their care. These children are sometimes known as the 'white stolen generation'. When resources in the form of financial support from the Federal Government became available in 1973, the number of adoptions reduced dramatically.

As yet, no federal apology has been made to those affected by this policy, although there has already been an apology from the Western Australian government and a federal apology will no doubt follow eventually.

We know that the outcomes for those affected by this policy have also been long term grief and loss. Much of our knowledge about this grief and loss has come from the agencies which have helped to support those affected. Post-adoption services have existed to provide support and professional counselling in Australia for more than thirty years. There are and have also been many adoption support groups which have existed throughout this period. These organisations have made an enormous contribution to the well-being of those affected by adoption separation.

Considering the huge reduction in the number of adoptions taking place over the last forty years, it is clear that the clientele seeking support from these organisations comes largely from the period when the number of adoptions was much higher. This highlights the long term nature of their grief and loss issues. There is no evidence to suggest that, had these adoptions been managed differently, the long term outcomes would have been any less severe, either for adults who were adopted as children or for their original parents.

Vulnerable children are no longer brought to Australia under child migrant schemes. Aboriginal children are no longer removed from their families in the way that the Stolen Generations were. Children removed from their families under child protection legislation are now able to be cared for in families under permanent guardianship orders, which allow children to retain their identities and their legal status within their families of origin. Few Australian children are adopted in the twenty-first century, because adoption is widely considered not to be in the best interests of children.

Then and now

When Australian children are considered to be unsafe living with their parents, we care for them, in Australia, as best we can. Child protection is, of course, a complex area and must be subject to constant, rigorous scrutiny, to ensure that it does, indeed, provide the best protection for children at risk.

Children are dependent and vulnerable, in every country. Children in countries outside of Australia are no less precious than Australian children. The Australian government has the responsibility of applying the same protections to children in other countries that they do to Australian-born children. If adoption is no longer considered to be in the best interests of Australian children, there is no justification for policies and practices which treat children in other countries with any less care and concern.

Australia has recognised that the injustices suffered by unsupported, unmarried mothers in the twentieth century resulted in family breakdowns which were not in the best interests of many mothers and their children. The federal government, therefore, has a moral responsibility to ensure not only that children are not being removed from their countries of origin through corrupt practices, such as child trafficking, but also that Australia is not supporting the social pressures which are currently being applied to facilitate the unnecessary removal of children from vulnerable mothers in other countries.

Less affluent countries are now being deemed incompetent because of their lack of resources, just as Australian single mothers were in the twentieth century and they are being punished, as those mothers were, by having their children removed from their care. In the same way that the number of adoptions in Australia reduced markedly after the introduction of the Sole Parent Pension in 1973, it is likely that if affluent countries like Australia provided information, support and resources to less affluent countries, we would see a dramatic reduction in the number of intercountry adoptions. Instead, we are continuing to create an 'intercountry stolen generation'.

ADOPTION SEPARATION

Countries which have lost children through intercountry adoption will have to deal with the personal and communal grief which results from this.

No doubt, in time to come, they will experience the same sequence of events which we have witnessed in Australia. They will set up support services to assist those who have experienced adoption separation; this has already happened in Korea. They will put a stop to intercountry adoption; this has already happened in Romania.

Eventually, they will recognise the long term impact of the policies and practices which allowed those family separations to occur and they will deliver apologies, as we have done in Australia.

Many Australians are ashamed and angered that children are being removed from their families, their communities, their heritage, their language and their countries of origin, to be adopted into Australian families. Australian children do not suffer those losses and we have no right to inflict them on children born in other countries. As a caring, responsible nation, we have no justification for facilitating intercountry adoption, as we have a responsibility to learn from the mistakes of the past and not to repeat them. Apologies may appear to be empty and meaningless, if they are not followed by genuine change.

In the near future, the Australian Government will doubtless be apologising to the *Intercountry Stolen Generation.*

The Times They Are A-Changin'

Who would have thought that a mother who had been separated from her child by adoption would be sitting in a Parliament building, with other mothers, who had also experienced adoption separation, looking and listening, as politicians wept while describing our loss and grief?

In 1970, when my son, Stephen, was born and adopted, I dreamt that one day he would sit by my side. Little did I imagine that, on the 19th of October 2010, in Western Australia, we would stand side by side and applaud as the Premier of Western Australia apologised for the past adoption policies and practices which separated so many mothers from their children. This was the first apology of its kind in the world and I am so happy that Stephen and I were able to be there together. It certainly was a memorable occasion.

The first government apology in Australia was the federal apology to the Stolen Generations in February, 2008. This was a momentous event for all Australians and the country virtually came to a standstill, to allow everyone to view the apology live on television. I was not able to be present in Parliament for that apology, but I was present for the apology to the Forgotten Australians and the British Child Migrants, which took place in Canberra, in November, 2009. I know from talking to the people who were there how moved they were that their issues were being recognised and that the government had decided to say 'sorry' for what had happened to them in the past. Both apologies included a recognition of the damage which had occurred and funding for services to address that damage.

Nothing that is said now can change what happened in the past for any of us, but these apologies have not only drawn the

245

attention of both the nation and the world to the issues involved, but are also an acknowledgement on the part of the government that past policies and practices were harmful and inappropriate.

Adoption in Australia has always been managed separately by each state. The apology in Western Australia came about because a mother who had been separated from her child by adoption approached her Member of Parliament, David Templeman, MP, Member for Mandurah and explained to him how her life had been affected by the separation from her child. She and other mothers continued to press for an official acknowledgment of the role of government in separating families. They had the support of many others, both around Australia and around the world.

It was a lovely, sunny day in Perth on the 19th of October and almost two hundred people gathered outside Parliament House to attend the apology. Before we went into the building, there was a small ceremony in the sunken garden where we acknowledged all those whose lives had been affected by adoption separation around the world and those who were deceased. Flowers were laid and balloons were released in honour of those not present. There was a warm, strong feeling of understanding and togetherness. Mention was made of the value of support groups and of the need for specialist services to address adoption-related issues. These were matters which I raised after the apology with politicians. I was assured that they are aware of the need for services to be adequately funded and for professionals to be appropriately trained and educated in adoption separation issues.

There were many representatives of the media present and the apology was given very good coverage in newspapers, on television and on the radio. We entered the Parliament building and made our way to the public gallery, which had seating for only a hundred and six people. Another room was set up where the others could watch on closed circuit television. The chamber was very attractive, with beautiful stained glass windows.

We waited anxiously through the end of Question Time, unsure of exactly what form the apology would take. We were told afterwards that the parliamentary web site almost went into meltdown, as so many people around the world logged on to watch the apology live.

The Premier of Western Australia, Colin Barnett, MP, moved the motion, which afterwards was carried unanimously, to apologise sincerely and unequivocally to those who had been adversely affected by past adoption policies and practices, which had not struck a balance between caring for the well-being of the mother and the well-being of the child. He acknowledged that some of the processes involved in past adoptions, especially between the 1940s and the 1980s, such as removing babies from their mothers after birth, had caused long term anguish and suffering and that the government was responsible for allowing this to happen. He mentioned the fact that many unmarried mothers were pressured into agreeing to adoption, at a time when they were emotionally vulnerable and that the events surrounding the births of their children had lasting consequences for them and their families. He said that for some mothers this had resulted in a 'deep and profound sadness' and that some had been 'severely scarred for decades to come'. He apologised unreservedly on behalf of the government to the mothers, the children and their respective extended families, whose interests were not best served by such policies and practices.

The Premier pointed out that these policies and practices occurred under past governments and that *they were wrong*. He applauded mothers for being 'survivors' and for having the courage to persist with their cause until this apology took place. He acknowledged that an apology cannot repair the damage, but hoped that it would assist in the healing process and offered the compassion and recognition of the Parliament.

The Premier also talked about those who were adopted and explained that their mothers did not cast them aside thoughtlessly, but cared deeply about their well-being. Many unmarried mothers in the twentieth century acted in ignorance of the consequences and so did not give informed consents to adoption. On that day in Western Australia, their motherhood was publicly honoured, at last.

The motion was passed unanimously and the Parliament said clearly, *We are sorry*. Other politicians also spoke. Some wept openly as they talked about our loss and grief and some of them disclosed adoption experiences within their own families. We applauded every politician who spoke, spontaneously disregarding the signs telling us that applause was not allowed. There was a great atmosphere of caring and support in the Parliament and some of the politicians met with us afterwards. When David Templeman, MP spoke, he called for both a state and a national enquiry and was given a standing ovation from the public gallery. I was so proud to have my son rise to his feet and applaud enthusiastically by my side.

We shared the experience with family members affected by adoption separation who had travelled from around Australia and with many more around the world who made contact before and after the apology. Our thoughts were also with others, who did not live to share this experience with us.

Afterwards, there was a great feeling of relief and appreciation from everyone present, that someone had finally listened and was prepared to declare publicly their concern for our suffering. Many of us felt as if our ship had finally come in and that we had at last been able to throw off the chains of shame and blame, which had bound us for so many years. We were inspired by the dedication and passion which had brought about this apology. We left Parliament House with the hope that this apology will be followed by many more.

I believe that the apology in Western Australia will not only help many people with their individual healing, but will also increase community awareness of the issues that many of us have had to deal with since our children were taken from us to be adopted. I have heard from many, many mothers around the world who are heartened by news of the Western Australian apology. This comment is very typical: *I can't tell you how it soothes a damaged heart to hear that at last there is some recognition of the suffering of mothers, fathers and children involved in adoption. My ambition now is to live long enough to see an apology given in Great Britain.* I share her ambition.

We have been told that other states and territories in Australia are now also considering apologising and many of us have drawn the attention of our own state and territory governments to the fact that the apology has taken place in Western Australia. There have also been discussions with the federal government and they are currently considering what would need to happen before a federal apology could be given.

I believe that Australia is setting an example and I hope that other countries will follow our lead.

One mother who was present expressed her feelings to me afterwards: *To receive this apology in such a public way enables me to feel regarded, that I matter, that what I went through has been acknowledged and wrong. This gift restores my dignity and self worth. I received a sincere apology and was told that my consent was **not** really given, because it was not an informed one; and that what happened was not my fault. So much was affirmed and validated and I feel empowered.*

This is a huge achievement and an example to the world. I believe that it is the start of a widespread acknowledgement of the loss and grief that were caused by past policies and practices and hopefully this will increase awareness of our issues in the community and help many to heal from the hurts of the past.

About the author

Evelyn Robinson, MA, Dip Ed, BSW, has both personal and professional experience of adoption separation and reunion. Evelyn gave birth to her son, Stephen, in Edinburgh, Scotland, in 1970 and he was adopted soon after his birth. Stephen and Evelyn were reunited in 1991 in Australia and continue to enjoy a close relationship. Evelyn has also been a professional social worker since 1996 and has been employed since that time as a counsellor and educator in the post-adoption field. She has always given generously of her time and energy to promote healing for those who have been separated by adoption and to educate the community around the long term outcomes of adoption separation. Evelyn has travelled to all of the countries represented in this book, in her own time and at her own expense, providing training and information sessions to members of the adoption community, professionals, government departments and adoption support organisations. Her books inform the work of professionals around the world and are used as self-help manuals by those who have experienced adoption separation. Through her international presentations and her books, Evelyn has made an enormous contribution to increasing awareness around the world of Australia's enlightened approach to adoption separation and reunion, now widely respected and envied. Evelyn is currently a member of the National Inter Country Adoption Advisory Group which meets regularly with the Australian Attorney-General's Department, to advise on intercountry adoption policy and practice. Further information about Evelyn Robinson and her invaluable work is available from www.clovapublications.com.